The Way of the Catalyst

How leaders create ***meaningful impact*** *without being consumed in the process*

Mais Alhasan

Rethink

First published in Great Britain in 2025
by Rethink Press (www.rethinkpress.com)

Disclaimer

The contents of this book are intended for educational purposes only. The content is not a substitute for professional medical advice, diagnosis, or treatment. Always consult a qualified healthcare provider regarding any physical or mental health condition. Reliance on any information provided herein is solely at your own risk.

This book is a work of nonfiction. Some stories are based on real events and lived experiences, while others are imagined or adapted. All are intended to serve the reader's learning and transformation journey. In certain cases, identifying details have been modified to preserve confidentiality or to support the narrative flow.

This book is offered in the spirit of growth and contribution. May it inspire clarity, courage, and meaningful change in your life.

Contents

Introduction

This book is for you—the leader, coach, consultant, change agent, politician, professional, parent, teacher, learner, or organizational influencer. The demands on you are high, and you probably wouldn't want it any other way. People like you are often looking for ways to manage pressures and honor commitments without making unnecessary compromises.

Whether you're navigating the complexities of corporations, governments, healthcare, education, communities, coaching, or parenting, your attitudes and the choices you make today set the tone for what comes next. The ripple effect you create influences the world around you in ways you may not even be aware of, impacting others' thoughts, behaviors, and attitudes, and contributing to a culture that defines the quality of life of everyone within it.

The Way of the Catalyst helps you amplify and choreograph those ripples. By becoming aware of your impact and learning how to direct it, guided by your big picture and your attitudes, you can live a rich and fulfilling life, making it easier on you and those around you.

Merriam-Webster defines a "catalyst" as: "A substance that enables a chemical reaction to proceed at a usually faster rate or under different conditions (as at a lower temperature) than otherwise possible."[1]

In chemistry, a catalyst accelerates a reaction without being consumed or permanently altered in the process. Similarly, people who act as catalysts bring clarity and forward momentum to even the most challenging of situations—through their presence and intentional choice of words, thoughts, and actions. They create impact with grace, while preserving their integrity under pressure.

I stumbled onto the lived experience of catalysis and cultural transformation while building BFL Group, a family business that began as a dream and evolved into a billion-dollar enterprise. As a founding member, I spent nearly two decades coaching teams and individuals, guiding them through the intricacies of growth and transformation.

Before we started BFL Group, my only experience in retail was going to the mall. My education didn't cover anything related to business. What I did have was a deep interest in people: what drives them, what drains them, why they do what they do, what brings them lasting joy, and how they can become the best version of themselves.

As a team, we were committed to bringing out the best in ourselves and each other, which allowed us to collaborate and grow together. We built a culture of truth, meaning, and lasting joy. It wasn't just about completing projects or achieving goals; it was about who we became in the process, both individually and as a team. We became "culture catalysts."

It took years of observation, study, and lived experience to uncover the key factor that makes some individuals not only successful, but also deeply respected and genuinely loved by those in their orbit. The subtle but powerful ingredient is their attitudes, a living filter through which they interpret and respond to the world. They inform their choices, color their interactions, and shape the energy they bring into every moment. Attitudes are the central focus of this book.

The attitudes and traits that make up catalysis are expressed in small, everyday encounters, even when no one is watching. They show up in the corridors of office buildings, in living rooms, at supermarket checkouts, and in offices both big and small. When you live with intention toward your attitudes, every moment becomes an opportunity to embody the Way of the Catalyst.

When I was thirty-seven years old, my dentist and dear family friend, Dr. A, told me that I had a tumor surrounding a wisdom tooth that never broke through the gum on my left jaw. Although it caused some damage to the jawbone, such tumors are mostly benign, and so was mine. The concern was that the tooth's roots were wrapped around the main nerve of my jaw. Removing the tooth and the tumor surrounding it risked damaging the nerve, which would cause a complete loss of sensation in the left side of my face.

Dr. A helped me find the best surgeon for this kind of procedure, who was based in New York. Before I traveled for the surgery, Dr. A said to me, "Mais, this is one of the best surgeons in the world for this. When you go to see him, he is going to explain what he will do during the surgery. He will lay out the risks. You need to hold it together and let him know that you trust him and know you are in safe hands. Let him go into the surgery knowing that you trust he will do the best he can. This will have an impact on him."

It took me a moment to process what he said, because it challenged my unconscious assumption that it is the doctor's role to reassure the patient. I thought, "That's a good example of a catalytic response." Dr. A had brought to my attention that emotional support is not solely the doctor's responsibility. The patient's attitude and behavior have an impact on the doctor, too.

I woke up after the surgery with a stabbing pain in my jaw, tears welling up in my eyes. The doctor came closer, looked me in the eyes, and said, "Are you in pain?" I could not make a sound, so I just nodded slightly. He smiled and said, "Congrats! That's good news. Your nerve is intact."

Deep in my heart, I know that this amazing surgeon would have done a fantastic job anyway, but maybe my attitude made it slightly easier for him.

Across much of the world, education systems still fall short in teaching life skills that could meaningfully shape children's futures—skills like emotional mastery, social intelligence, stress management, mind–body awareness, and the art of communication, negotiation, and influence. While academic subjects like math, science, and language dominate the curriculum, mental and emotional development often takes a back seat. In many cases, discipline and compliance are prioritized over inner resilience and personal growth.

As a result, children grow into adults with insufficient tools to navigate their inner and outer environments. This often leads to ineffective dynamics in relationships, strained family connections, and dysfunctional workplace cultures, ultimately resulting in a decline in overall well-being and productivity.

This book is about returning to the basics—your attitudes and the tools that bring them to life. You are invited to embrace the ideas, adapt them to your unique context, and use them to spark meaningful change in your world. Whether or not you hold formal authority, whether you're engaged in the social or professional realm, and whatever your age or position, this book is for you.

The Way of the Catalyst journey begins in Part One with Chapter One: Change and Chapter Two: The Big Picture Personal Canvas. We start by examining deliberate and incidental change, along with the tools to navigate them effectively. From there, we explore the four building blocks of the Big Picture Personal Canvas©, followed by a practical framework to help you design your own.

Part Two focuses on the Five Attitudes of the Catalyst, each represented by a reference letter:

- **R** for Responsibility
- **P** for Proactivity
- **I** for Interdependence
- **F** for Influence
- **X** for Excellence

Each attitude is expressed through three distinct traits, noted as R1, R2, R3 for Responsibility, and similarly for the others. The attitudes in *The Way of the Catalyst* are defined as follows:

1. **Responsibility:** Taking charge of inner thoughts, emotions, and stories (Chapter Three).
2. **Proactivity:** Living life by design (Chapter Four).
3. **Interdependence:** Sharing power with all involved (Chapter Five).
4. **Influence:** Causing an effect without force (Chapter Six).
5. **Excellence:** Bringing the dynamic self, moment to moment (Chapter Seven).

Part Three uncovers the stories of two catalysts who are living examples of the concepts in this book: Zimmy, "The Catalyst Next Door" (Chapter Eight), and Michel, "The Catalyst Leader" (Chapter Nine). We wrap up with practical application in Chapter Ten: Becoming the Catalyst.

By the end of *The Way of the Catalyst,* you will be able to create your own Big Picture Personal Canvas—your North Star for clear direction and deliberate decision-making. You will also have the tools to embody the Five Attitudes of the Catalyst, enabling you to live a rich and fulfilling life, while making it easier on yourself and those around you.

PART ONE
THE CATALYST'S FUNDAMENTALS

Change is no longer a seasonal event. It's the atmosphere in which we live. Whether it's subtle or earth-shattering, welcome or disruptive, change is happening. In the midst of it, we're required not only to adapt, but to evolve—to learn and expand ourselves—in order to advance our life experience. Part One lays the foundation for doing exactly that.

We begin by reframing change not as something that happens to us, but as something we can engage with intentionally. Instead of resisting, chasing, or fearing it, what if you could relate to change with presence—as a partner in your growth? The first chapter explores the nature of change and how our response to it shapes our experience. You'll learn the tools to navigate change with a new level of awareness and intent.

From there, we move into the core anchoring tool of *The Way of the Catalyst*: your Big Picture Personal Canvas. This isn't a typical life plan or performance goal; it's a multidimensional reflection of what truly matters to you, not just what you want to do, but who you want to be and how you want to live.

Your Big Picture Personal Canvas helps you map your personal landscape across four essential dimensions: Physical, Emotional, Mental, and Social (PEMS). These aren't separate compartments; they're interwoven layers of your lived experience. When they align, life flows more easily for you and those around you. When they don't, friction shows up, often as burnout, confusion, or dissatisfaction.

The canvas doesn't promise instant transformation. It invites you into a deeper level of clarity, anchored in self-honesty and inner congruence. You'll begin to see where your energy leaks, what drives your decisions, and how your sense of direction can become more intentional.

Together, these two chapters are not about fixing yourself; they are about remembering yourself at your best. They point you toward identifying what's real, what's possible, and what's truly worth your time, energy, and presence.

This is the groundwork for becoming a catalyst—someone who makes a meaningful impact with less pressure and without getting consumed in the process. Someone who creates gracefully with ease and preserves their integrity and harmony under pressure.

Let's begin.

1
Change

Change doesn't always knock; sometimes it kicks down the door and makes itself at home. In this chapter, we'll explore two fundamental types of change: the type that you invite (deliberate) and the type that imposes itself on you (incidental). You'll then be introduced to a framework designed to help you recognize and navigate the call for change when it arrives.

We'll also explore three levels of awareness in relation to time, along with the concept of Integrated Time Awareness (ITA). Then, we'll take a closer look at the skill of zooming in and zooming out of situations to enhance your ITA in practice. Finally, we'll unpack a real-life example of how attitudes are shaped and reinforced from the earliest days of life.

Change: Deliberate or incidental

We humans are not programmed to notice subtle changes as they happen. You probably look in the mirror every day, but you only notice how you're aging when you see an old photo. Likewise, children grow and change rapidly, but we only see it when we realize the shoes and clothing we bought just a few months ago are now too small.

In an advertisement called "The Attention Test", the Škoda Fabia car is shown parked on a street in West London.[2] The narrator tells the audience that they are testing how much attention the "attention-stealing" design of the new Škoda Fabia actually steals. The screen blinks once every four seconds, but no passers-by stop to look at the car, despite its attractive features and "fresh sporty look." Messages appear at the bottom of the screen to prompt the viewer: "Keep watching closely, you won't believe what happens," and "Think nothing's happening?"

In under a minute, after the screen has blinked thirteen times, the speaker points out that the entire street has changed right before the viewer's eyes without them noticing. Then, the ad concludes with a funny statement that plays on our change blindness: "So there we have it: proof that the new Škoda Fabia is truly attention-stealing."

This ad reveals a simple yet profound truth: when your attention is locked on one focal point, your mind naturally filters out everything else. You become blind to details and events happening right before your eyes because you're not looking for them when your mind is focused on something else. Your eyes don't just see what is there; they follow your mind's lead in what to focus on, consciously or unconsciously.

Change is even more subtle when it comes to life experiences that shape your character. Usually, people who are practiced in introspection and self-reflection can spot inner changes more easily than others. You probably recognize how your interactions with others and your understanding of situations have evolved over time. Although the solid core within remains constant and unchangeable, how you express it and the impact you make with it can be fine-tuned, or even transformed.

While incidental change is an unplanned occurrence, deliberate change is the result of intentional action and practice, guided by a clear vision of a desired outcome. Both have an impact on life experience and drive what comes next.

Incidental change is triggered by external factors, including loss, bereavement, divorce, health conditions, redundancy, inflation, and market crises, among others. The sudden, dramatic changes caused by the pandemic in 2020 highlighted the importance of inner resilience, emotional mastery, effective relationships, and agile thinking on a personal level. At an organizational level, companies that fostered a healthy, strong culture were able to navigate change relatively well, continuing to deliver during the global crisis without placing unnecessary pressure on their people.

Deliberate change is self-initiated and includes personal development, therapy, career change, entering into or leaving a relationship, market expansion, mergers and acquisitions, and cultural transformation, for example.

The Way of the Catalyst engages change, even the incidental kind, with intent. Catalysts are consistently aware of how they tackle change and the trail they leave behind in the process. For them, the outcome of change is consciously driven, regardless of the scenario and whether they initiate it or actively participate in it.

The call for change

Every call for change, even when it's incidental, presents an opportunity. In a culture of Catalysts, this call is answered, and the greatest achievement is who they become in the process, individually and as a team.

Many organizations have paid a heavy price for resisting change. They suffered bankruptcy, lost market dominance, or lost market share. This can be seen in Kodak's failure to embrace digital photography, Nokia's delay in adopting smartphone technology, Blackberry's resistance to touchscreen, and the numerous retail businesses that failed to adapt to the rise of e-commerce.

At an individual level, the call for change is usually more obvious; for example, when your job has become deadening, a relationship has run its course, or your body is sending signals that there's something wrong. This may manifest as restlessness, dissatisfaction, frustration, a decline in energy, procrastination, physical pain, or feedback from others that hits a nerve or reveals a blind spot. These indicators are hard to miss. They might be ignored, overlooked, or suppressed, but they don't go away. They persist until you do something about them.

The Way of the Catalyst is to answer these calls for change before they spawn problems, like an innocent-looking egg in a horror film that eventually hatches a monster. You have an inner sense of when advancement is necessary to sustain what you have already built and to evolve to the next level, perhaps by expanding your skill set, acting on a long-standing matter, starting therapy, or changing your lifestyle.

Acting upon internal and external calls for change requires mental agility and connecting with the demands of present reality instead of reverting to old patterns of thought, attitudes, and behaviors. Add to this, of course, brutal self-honesty. This is as true for individuals as it is for communities and organizations.

A good starting point is to become clear on what problem you need to solve or what question you need to answer by engaging in a process of discovery and exploration before deciding on a course of action. Solving surface-level problems drains your time and energy because it leads you to constantly fight fires instead of preventing them. Investing the necessary time in thoughtful assessment helps you gain clarity on the root of the problem, allowing you to strategically design a plan that leads to meaningful, lasting change.

The call for change framework

Change is crazy and not necessarily subtle. It can set your house on fire to force you out. It is often uncomfortable even when you are actively seeking it. However, it is part of life, and it will happen whether you think you're ready or not. It can take place gracefully and elegantly, or with you kicking and screaming. How you go about change is your choice.

At some point in the evolution of BFL Group, we hit a brick wall. We had trained pricing officers for each category and brand according to set guidelines, which worked well for the first three stores. However, as the business grew, we started to notice price discrepancies, sometimes even in the same store.

A friend and business associate suggested that we automate the process, which seemed like a major challenge, given the wide variety of merchandise and incomplete product series. But we knew it had to be done if we were to expand. The process started with a call for change (price discrepancies), followed by deliberate change (a series of action steps) to bring about a specific outcome (automated pricing system) for a specific purpose (expanding the business).

Drawing from this example and others, I developed a simple eight-step framework for navigating any call for change, whether incidental or deliberate. To illustrate it, I use the case of price discrepancies at BFL retail stores:

1. What problem are you solving/What question are you answering?

Discrepancies in pricing caused by human error or differing interpretations among members of the pricing team.

2. What other problems/questions are relevant to this and causing the same pressure/impact?

Frequent customer complaints and significant time wasted by both store and warehouse teams, who are forced to correct pricing errors and address issues with the customers.

3. How did this start?

Early on, we developed pricing guidelines organized by category and brand, and trained a team of pricing officers to implement them. The issue of price discrepancies became apparent during our transition from a small to a medium-sized business.

4. What is your clear intent? (Identify the desired change in clear, specific terms.)

Our intent was to open two to three new stores each year. To achieve that growth, we needed a fully automated pricing process that would ensure accuracy, consistency, and efficiency to reduce manual errors and free up our people's time for more meaningful work.

5. Apply the stop, keep, and start (SKS) model by Phil Daniels:[3]

- What do you need to **S**top doing?

  Relying on a manual pricing process.

- What do you need to **K**eep doing?

  Applying manual pricing until formulas are developed and integrated into the system.

- What do you need to **S**tart doing?

  Analyzing each individual product line, developing pricing formulas, feeding them into the system, testing their accuracy, and phasing out manual pricing.

6. What are the short-term benefits? What are the long-term ones?

Short-term benefits included reduced pricing errors, fewer customer complaints, and effective use of our people's time and energy. Long-term benefits included greater scalability and improved data analysis and forecasting.

7. What actions can you take now?

Prioritize high-volume categories, assign a dedicated lead to oversee the process, and run a time trial for automating the first product line to estimate the overall completion date.

Of course, it is one thing to have a plan and completely another to execute it, which is why you need a final, "ongoing" step...

8. Effective and dynamic identification, utilization, and expansion of resources.

We regularly identified human, technical, and procedural resources that were needed at each phase of the process.

It took us an entire year, but with the support of our committed team, we did it. We learned that taking timely, intentional action built momentum and that resources and opportunities started to emerge as we moved forward. By answering that call for change, we exponentially increased market share and created job opportunities for thousands. Today, the company stands as the leading discount retailer in the region, with over 130 stores across the Middle East and Southeast Asia.

When you welcome change with an open heart and a curious mind, it will show you the way, one step at a time.

Levels of awareness: Integrated Time Awareness (ITA)

It may seem obvious that the past is behind us, the present is unfolding now, and the future holds possibilities yet to come. Yet, we often carry unconscious biases in how we relate to time. Our attention tends to gravitate toward one specific time orientation—past, present, or future—and that focus shapes our thoughts, feelings, behaviors, and attitudes. That's why it's worth placing our time biases under the microscope… or perhaps the hourglass.

Awareness of the past

Awareness of the past is shaped by the experiences, feelings, and events that we've already lived through. But there's a paradox: memory is inherently unreliable. We tend to over-emphasize extreme events, whether positive or negative, while filtering out details that do not align with our overall perception of the event. Numerous studies on the fallibility of eyewitness testimony reinforce the idea that simply having lived through something doesn't mean we hold the final truth about it.

When an awareness of the past is dominant, people often repeat the same stories, reinforcing the subconscious beliefs shaped by those experiences, whether constructive or destructive. You'll notice them doing things the same old way, even when it's no longer helpful. That's because we naturally gravitate toward what's familiar. The primitive brain equates familiarity with safety and instinctively steers us away from the unknown to protect us from potential threats. But this survival mechanism can backfire, causing people to stay stuck in a rut and repeat old patterns in relationships, at work, within communities, and in outcomes over and over again.

A fixation on our awareness of the past creates what I call the "replica state," a state of being where the person does not recognize that their past is controlling their present and shaping their future.

Awareness of the present

An awareness of the present is rooted in the here and now, free from past memories or future concerns. It is marked by a sense of novelty, where we experience life detached from traumas, fears, or even desires and dreams.

When an awareness of the present is dominant, people express curiosity about others, situations, or new learnings. They move from one experience to another, often without attachment or direction. They may come across as light, carefree, and fun to be around. In its functional form, the person is described as Zen, grounded, and relaxed. In its dysfunctional form, the person may be perceived as inconsistent, restless, or lacking purpose.

A fixation on an awareness of the present creates what I call the "wanderer state," a state of being where the person drifts freely through life without a clear sense of direction or destination. In this state, the past may be suppressed, along with the lessons it holds, while the future may feel irrelevant or unreachable, limiting one's ability to design a meaningful path forward.

Awareness of the future

An awareness of the future is shaped by a range of possibilities, filtered through both conscious and unconscious beliefs. It acts as a lens that colors our perception of what life may bring.

When an awareness of the future is dominant, people indulge in dreams, fantasizing about a different reality while overlooking the opportunities and challenges right in front of them. This focus often serves as an escape from a hard-to-tolerate reality into a fantasy world. You might observe them making decisions disconnected from their current situation, discounting both the significance of the obstacles they face and the options available to address them. They may come across as detached or even delusional. They live in a world that exists only in their head, with little to no deliberate action to bring their vision to life.

This fixation on an awareness of the future is often called being in "la-la land"—a state I refer to as the "la-la state," where the head is in the clouds but the feet are not on the ground. In this state, creative thinking is compromised, and the ability to bridge the gap between our current reality and a desired future becomes blurred.

What is Integrated Time Awareness?

The Way of the Catalyst is to recognize that no single level of awareness—past, present, or future—is helpful on its own for the long term. Catalysts are adept at harnessing the lessons from the past to effect change in the present, guided by a future vision that is dynamic and constantly evolving. In *The Way of the Catalyst*, this concept is called Integrated Time Awareness (ITA).

ITA is the practice of fully engaging in the present moment, grounded in wisdom drawn from past experiences and leveraging both inner and outer resources to shape an elevated reality guided by an intentional big picture.

There are ever-increasing demands on our attention. We face countless insignificant distractions and insufficient mental energy to take everything in, let alone process it. We can add to that the memories of a redundant past, the challenges of a limiting present, and the uncertainties of an unfolding future. Amid such currents, developing the ability to consciously focus our attention and integrate our awareness becomes a pure expression of inner freedom.

Several years ago, I attended a leadership retreat in Spain, located on a mountainside surrounded by expansive land, where we went for hikes and practiced our morning routine of stretching, meditation, and setting intentions for the day.

One morning, the two program leaders announced that we were to venture into nature without our watches, mobile phones, or any electronics. They did not specify exactly how long we were to stay away. Each of us was asked to choose a spot where no one else was visible and to remain there in silence, simply observing our surroundings. We were to return to the retreat center when we heard the sound of drums.

We were tasked with contemplating the question, "When does something come to life, and when does it cease to exist?" I don't know how many hours passed before it became clear to me. The answer had to do with my attention. Whenever I recognized the existence of a bird, a flower, or a tree, it became alive in my awareness. Whenever my attention shifted elsewhere, it ceased to exist, at least for me.

There is an exchange of energy when we make contact with something or someone physically, emotionally, or mentally. Catalysts are discerning about who or what they transact their energy with. For them, the past is a learning experience that they appreciate. They focus on elements that matter in the present to progress toward a desired future, guided by their big picture, which encompasses fundamental aspects of their life: Physical, Emotional, Mental, and Social (or PEMS—more on this in the next chapter, The Big Picture Personal Canvas).

Let's now explore a crucial skill that allows catalysts to maintain their ITA.

Zooming in and zooming out

Like a camera lens, this is your ability to view close matters from a distance (the big picture perspective or zooming out) and distant matters close up (the micro perspective or zooming in), noticing the small details that line up to form the greater whole.

Imagine looking out of a third-floor window. You would likely see people passing by, trees lining each side of the road, streetlights spaced evenly along the median of a two-way street, and storefronts and coffee shops along the way. The details would appear relatively clear.

Now imagine observing the same scene from the thirtieth floor. The small details would be harder to distinguish, but the higher vantage point would reveal far more—small side roads, a roundabout at a distant intersection, a bridge connecting your street to a national highway, and so on.

Navigating your personal and professional life works much the same way. Have you ever struggled to craft a solution from the information immediately available to you? Maybe your creativity was compromised by the rising pressure of not seeing a way out. If you remain stuck at the third-floor perspective, you might come up with a partial fix that proves ineffective over the long run. What you would need to do is zoom out.

Developing the mental agility to zoom in and out of situations takes practice. It takes a moment of quiet observation for ITA to kick in. You need to bring relevant lessons from the past (zoom out), recognize the call for change in the moment (zoom in), define the destination (zoom out again), then navigate the path (zoom back in). And repeat. It's a dynamic, ongoing process that spirals upward and onward in a progressive, expansive movement toward effective change and growth.

In mergers and acquisitions, the integration process often dilutes the acquired company's culture, identity, and practices in the pursuit of unification. However, Bob Iger, Disney's former CEO, took a distinct approach marked by leadership excellence, long-term vision, and lateral thinking.

Disney had a distribution agreement for funding and distributing Pixar films, while retaining ownership and sequel rights. Friction began to surface when Steve Jobs, Pixar's CEO at the time, perceived the agreement as unfair and shut down negotiations to renew the deal with Disney.

When Bob Iger stepped into the CEO role in 2005, Disney and Pixar had been trying—and failing—to negotiate a new agreement for four years. Iger understood that the rise of new technology would make Disney's traditional animation obsolete in no time. He orchestrated an acquisition deal that allowed Pixar autonomy and creative independence while benefiting from Disney's funding and resources.[4]

This decision combined Disney's vision and storytelling "soul" with Pixar's creativity and cutting-edge technology. The deal led to an extremely successful relationship that revolutionized the animation industry. It was only possible because Iger was able to zoom out to the thirtieth-floor perspective and see the bigger picture of the strategic acquisition and how to make it happen.

The path ahead

Later in this book, after crafting your Big Picture Personal Canvas, we will explore attitudes, which will take you back to basics. This work might seem simple, but is it easy? For most people, it is not quite. Why? Because attitudes often run on autopilot, and doing this work means making the unconscious conscious.

Attitudes are formed early in childhood through observing and experiencing the immediate world around us, such as family, school, friends, neighbors, and community. The attitudes, actions, and behaviors we witness in these environments shape our understanding of how the world works and our place in it. Unless conscious awareness intervenes, we either mirror the attitudes we observe, internalize those permitted or approved by parents or parent-like figures, or rebel against them by adopting their extreme opposites. In this way, the development of character is left to chance until the adult within chooses to shape an intentional way of being, free from the limitations of past experiences.

One beautiful summer day on a beach in southern France, I was mesmerized by the late-afternoon sunlight dancing across the water's surface, casting a glimmering path as if the sea had been dusted with diamond powder. That moment of tranquility was ruptured by someone loudly scolding a child.

Twenty meters away, a woman sat with two little girls, aged about nine and five years old. The five-year-old was throwing pebbles into the sea, watching the ripple effect. Her curiosity didn't stop there; she began to throw handfuls of pebbles, then graduated from pebbles to larger rocks. That's when the woman scolded her.

The little girl sat in silence, running her hand over the perfectly smooth pebbles. I wondered what was going through her head at that moment. If her curiosity was constantly suppressed, and she was repeatedly spoken to in a disrespectful manner, devoid of love and compassion, what attitudes might she internalize?

She might take on:

- The "observed attitude" of lack of Responsibility for thoughts and emotions: "You make me angry, and I will give you what you deserve."
- The "permitted attitude" of passivity (as opposed to Proactivity): "Don't think. Do as you are told."
- The "permitted attitude" of codependence (as opposed to Interdependence): "It is not OK to be different or want different things."
- The "observed attitude" of weak Influence: "To make change happen, use force."
- The "permitted attitude" of conformity (as opposed to Excellence): "Do not upset others; you are not important."

The woman might be a loving and caring parent who was having a bad day or simply operating out of habit. However, that does not negate the fact that her attitude may have caused harm or discomfort to those around her.

There are two determining factors that influence which attitudes the child will pick. First is the repetitiveness of the pattern demonstrated to the child, and the second is the child's perception, which is completely outside the parent or caregiver's control. That's how two children can grow up in the same household and have completely different sets of attitudes.

One positive attitude often generates another. A negative attitude, however, can generate either a positive or a negative attitude, depending on the meaning the child assigns to it. For example, the little girl on the beach might decide, "I don't like being talked to like this. I like it when people are kind." That small narrative could grow into an attitude of communicating with respect, love, and compassion. The power lies in the child's perception. Parents can influence it, but they cannot control it. The formation of negative attitudes can occur even in the most loving and well-intentioned of families.

As catalysts, we now know that the power lies within us, and we are free to operate consciously from that perspective. We can choose a positive output (our behavior), no matter the input (stimuli from the environment), to lead a rich and fulfilling life that is easy for us and others.

Catalysts accept the call for change, empowered by ITA, the inner agility to zoom in on and out of the moment, and a set of attitudes that allow for growth and transformation under milder conditions than would otherwise be possible.

The Way of the Catalyst brings unconscious patterns into conscious awareness and offers a roadmap to the Five Attitudes of the Catalyst that we introduced earlier:

1. **Responsibility:** Taking charge of inner thoughts, emotions, and stories.
2. **Proactivity:** Living life by design.
3. **Interdependence:** Sharing power with all involved.
4. **Influence:** Causing an effect without force.
5. **Excellence:** Bringing the dynamic self, moment to moment.

A baseline Culture Catalyst Self-Assessment is available online free of charge to measure your overall "perceived proficiency" in the Five Culture Catalyst Attitudes. There are five proficiency levels, with level five being the highest level of demonstrating each attitude constantly and consistently.

I invite you to take the assessment before exploring the tools in the coming chapters. You can find it at: https://ccp.riseleadership.me.

Key points

- Incidental change is an unplanned occurrence.
- Deliberate change is the result of intentional action and practice, guided by a clear vision of a desired outcome.
- Both incidental and deliberate change have an impact on life experience and drive what comes next.
- Catalysts answer the call for change, and their greatest achievement is who they become in the process, individually and as a collective.
- Once you engage in timely, intentional action, it gains momentum.
- Integrated Time Awareness (ITA) is the practice of fully engaging in the present moment, grounded in wisdom drawn from past experiences, and leveraging both inner and outer resources to shape an elevated reality guided by an intentional big picture.
- Zooming in and zooming out is the ability to see close matters from a distance and distant matters closely.

- Attitudes are formed early in childhood through observing and experiencing the immediate world around us.
- The power to choose our attitudes lies within us and is unlocked by bringing unconscious patterns into conscious awareness.

2

The Big Picture Personal Canvas

Think of the Big Picture Personal Canvas as an actual canvas that you can use to create your own unique masterpiece. The blank canvas fabric is "You," and the paint on the canvas is your "Social Space" (the world around you).

Your canvas consists of the three building blocks that make up "You": your Physical, Emotional, and Mental (PEM) dimensions. Your Social Space (S) is built on these. Your Social Space includes your family, work, friends, neighbors, and everyone and everything external with which you interact, impact, and which impacts you in return.

The interplay of the Physical, Emotional, Mental, and Social Space (PEMS) dimensions shapes your overall life experience. If the foundation is strong and well-maintained, you can build on it in a stable and sustainable manner. In other words, when your PEM aspects are well cared for, strengthened, and nurtured with sufficient depth, you have a steady ground that is reliable enough to hold everything else that rests on it—your Social Space (S), which is the interaction of your PEM with the outside world.

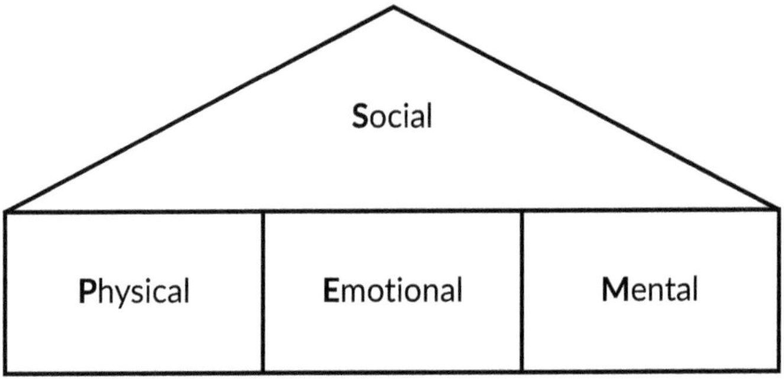

The Big Picture Personal Canvas of the Catalyst: PEMS dimensions

The Big Picture Personal Canvas is the launchpad that sets off the Catalyst's purpose of leading a rich and fulfilling life while making it easy on oneself and others.

We will look at each of the individual PEMS dimensions (Physical, Emotional, Mental, and the Social Space), and explore what a hyper-fixation on only one of these aspects to the exclusion of the others looks and sounds like. Then, we will examine the Big

Picture Personal Canvas framework, using an illustrative example.

The Physical (P)

The body is a marvelous network of interconnected functions and systems working in harmony. It does most of the work to keep you alive and well. Your part is simply giving your physical body the active attention it needs. It requires a sufficient investment of your time, intent, and energy to help create the conditions for its optimal functioning.

Certain areas need your constant and consistent care and maintenance:

- Nutrition and hydration
- Rest and repair
- Tenacity (stamina, endurance, strength)
- Flexibility (of joints, muscles, and spine)
- State of the vital and endocrine systems

Your relationship with your body, like any important relationship, needs attention, structure, and care to thrive. This book won't tell you what to eat, when to sleep, or how to exercise—there are experts for that. What matters here is creating a system that works for you, one that supports your energy, vitality, and long-term well-being. Maintaining your physical self-care helps prevent problems, or at least allows you to catch them early.

Think of your body as a friend who communicates with you in feedback loops. The relationship with the body is often overlooked, underestimated, or taken for granted until it sends a wake-up call that can no longer be ignored. Alfred Korzybski, a Polish-American scholar and the founder of general semantics, is attributed with having said the well-known quote, "God may forgive your sins, but your nervous system won't," referring to the lasting impact of stress, perception, and language on the human body (more on this in the next topics: the Emotional and the Mental). This phrase serves as a powerful reminder that our relationship with the body is often one-sided—we demand, suppress, and override, while the body continues to carry the burden without protest until it can no longer.

The body reacts eventually to how it is used or abused. It does not take into account intentions or excuses, such as: "I did this for my family," "I had to work hard," "I really wanted to do something but didn't know where to start," "I was busy," or "I didn't know." The "why" does not matter for the body. It operates with a binary understanding: your way of living either supports or compromises your health. This simplistic approach allows for a clear feedback loop, positive or negative.

The body is often the last to send a signal that something is wrong following earlier mental and emotional indicators, and it typically takes longer to heal. Any delay in addressing physical issues puts additional strain on the mental and emotional aspects.

CASE STUDY: Listening to the subtle signs

Ms. C was a forty-five-year-old entrepreneur with a tight schedule that led her to miss meals, work on weekends, and sleep only five hours a day (on good days). She was laser-focused on her vision for her company, which won her recognition and admiration. However, despite her rising success, she started to feel lethargic. She lost her inner motivation and drive and felt depressed for no apparent reason.

It reached a point where she became alarmed and contacted a friend who was a functional medicine doctor. Her friend ran some tests, and it turned out that Ms. C had severe deficiencies in some essential vitamins and minerals. She was prescribed the necessary dosage of supplements and advised to make major changes in her lifestyle. Her friend, the doctor, said, "Your body is sending a gentle message that you need to make some adjustments. The next message might not be as subtle."

Ms. C made a decision that day to give her health and her work equal importance, so that she could realize her dream while also being healthy and energized every step of the way. She took her friend's advice, made the necessary changes, and started to feel like herself again after four weeks of treatment and lifestyle changes.

Due to the time it can take to signal the alarm, the body is often taken for granted. The tricky part is that some feedback loops are instantaneous (if you jump off the first floor, you'll probably break some bones) while other feedback loops take hours (like food poisoning after eating bad food). Then there are the feedback loops that can take years, depending on the intensity of the imbalance, whether it's due to poor diet, insufficient rest, inadequate physical activity, or another similar oversight. Sometimes, by the time the body sets off an alarm, it is too late for a full recovery.

Fixation on the Physical

The Physical is the first building block of your Big Picture Personal Canvas. Exaggerated focus on the Physical can lead to a distorted sense of self-worth and vanity, a tendency to seek validation and recognition for superficial attractiveness, depression, dysfunctional attachments, unhealthy judgments, and addictive behavior.

This could manifest in a variety of ways that are unique to the person. Here are some of the most common:

- Over-indulgence in grooming and physical appearance
- Excessive training and workout routines
- Obsession with weight, body shape, and diets

- Addiction to plastic surgeries and quick fixes
- Compulsive shopping for fashion

The Way of the Catalyst is to honor and celebrate the body's ability and adaptability, finding joy in expanding its capability and feeling awe at its responsiveness and resilience. It's about prioritizing health and long-term functionality, where looking good is a byproduct of being well and feeling good in the body.

As a catalyst, you sustain a healthy lifestyle because of love and respect for your body, by investing time in activities like sport or movement that give you energy, eating food that nourishes your body, and making sacred your sleep time to allow your system to cleanse, recover, and repair. The aim is to curate a life experience that is rich, balanced, and joyful, filled with meaningful moments shared with those who matter the most, anchored in a sense of self-worth that does not depend on external validation but rather emanates from within.

The Emotional (E)

The Emotional is the second building block of your Big Picture Personal Canvas, linking the Physical (P) and the Mental (M). Emotions generate a visceral reaction (P) and also stimulate and fuel perception (M). In this section, you will discover how to process the physical side of emotions to calm the nervous system, using a *Vipassana*-based technique that is thousands of years old. *Vipassana* means "insightful observation" or "clear seeing" in the Pāli language. It involves the simple observation of emotions in the body without judgment or storytelling. Then, you will explore the mental processing of emotions using the RAHA technique, which brings deeper understanding and clarity.

Emotion is defined by the *American Psychological Association Dictionary* as: "A complex reaction pattern, involving experiential, behavioral, and physiological elements, by which an individual attempts to deal with a personally significant matter or event."[5]

"Complex" signifies that emotions are not simple or singular. "Reaction" implies there is no control over them. "Pattern" means that they are repetitive. Emotions are experienced in the body through the release of neurotransmitters and hormones that activate the autonomic nervous system, causing either a sympathetic (stress response) or parasympathetic (calm, peaceful, and relaxed response) state. This, in turn, triggers a behavior "to deal with a personally significant matter or event." In other words, it's only when you perceive something as important, whether positively or negatively, that you have an emotional reaction to it.

Emotions are a powerful source of creativity, inspiration, energy, motivation, and insight. They inform what is significant to you, and they need to be acknowledged and explored, but without becoming entangled in the stories that trigger them. It might seem that we have an innate tendency to avoid negative emotions and to seek positive ones. In reality, we seek what's familiar. We are driven by mental and emotional habits that color the lens through which we view ourselves, others, and the world around us. Mental and emotional habits, like any habits, can be changed.

In his book *Letting Go*, David Hawkins, an internationally known psychiatrist, author, and speaker, said:

> "To the fearful person, this world is a terrifying place. To the angry person, this world is a chaos of frustration and vexation. To the guilty person, it's a world of temptation and sin, which they see everywhere. What we are holding inside, colors our world."[6]

The Way of the Catalyst is to feel the emotions and transcend them. Catalysts are tuned in to their emotions; they welcome them all. They do not feel the need to suppress or avoid emotions because they know how to recover and process them gracefully. They experience the full range of emotions from an elevated space of trust in themselves and their power to co-create with life.

The Emotional (E) is a bridge that connects the Physical (P) and the Mental (M). Transcending an emotion requires processing both endpoints—the Physical (P) and the Mental (M)—to reach a state of nonattachment, by leveraging your power to harness the message in your emotions, in service of your big picture. In other words, it means making emotions work for you.

The terms "emotions" and "feelings" are often used interchangeably, but they are two different things. While emotions are visceral (originating in the body), feelings are the mental interpretations of these physical sensations. Interpretation is where your power lies, because it is within your control to change, adapt, and fine-tune.

The Physical endpoint: Processing emotions in the body

Name the feeling

When someone is asked, "What do you feel now?" they might say, "I'm hungry" (sensation), "I feel this is not working" (thought), or "I'm feeling down" (too generic, can mean lacking energy or motivation, which is a physical or mental state). None of these is a feeling.

Naming the feeling allows for clarity, as it acknowledges two parts of yourself. Let's name these two parts Y1 and Y2: Y1 experiences the emotion, and Y2 witnesses Y1 experiencing the emotion. One part of you is feeling; the other part is simply observing or witnessing. This process creates space between you and your emotion, allowing you access to an elevated part of yourself that's unattached to the emotion, which loosens the grip emotion has on you.

Gloria Willcox's Feeling Wheel is a great tool to help you name the feeling more specifically.[7] There are six primary feelings at the center (sad, angry, scared, peaceful, powerful, and joyful), and secondary and tertiary feelings radiating outward that help you identify the feeling more accurately.

Notice the sensation in your body

Observe where in your body you feel the emotion. Let go, for now, of the story of why you feel this way or what you're going to do about it. Simply observe. Notice the color, shape, size, texture, weight, and temperature of the feeling in your body. Notice any changes.

Stay with it quietly for 90 seconds. The neuroanatomist Dr. Jill Bolte Taylor found that 90 seconds is the physiological lifespan of an emotional response.[8] The emotion does not get stuck in the body; your body flushes it out naturally if you stop resisting and give it permission to do so by withholding any thoughts or inner narratives. Your body knows how to process it.

The 90-second rule works best when you catch the emotion early and allow yourself to process it. If you let it carry you into a downward spiral, it may take longer to work through.

Take long, deep breaths

Breathe deeply, holding your back straight and relaxing your shoulders. Research shows that hunching the back reduces lung capacity and stresses the heart. Breathing in and out through the nose, feel your lower abdominal muscles rising with the inhale and falling with the exhale. Start by emptying all the air from your lungs, then inhale for 5 seconds. Pause for 5 seconds, exhale for 8 seconds, and pause for 5 seconds before drawing another breath.

Ask for the message

Once the emotion decreases in intensity and feels small enough to figuratively fit in the palm of your hand, imagine holding it, and ask: "What message do you have for me?" Note down the first thing that comes up. It takes no longer than 3 to 7 seconds to get the message. Any longer than this, and it becomes a mental fabrication.

The Mental endpoint: RAHA technique

Raha in Arabic means comfort, rest, or relief. It helps in filtering the thoughts and ideas that come with the burst of an emotion, once the physiological reaction is processed. The purpose of the RAHA technique is to allow the mental space for you to connect with your big picture. RAHA stands for relevant, accurate, helpful, action.

Once your body is rebalanced, you are ready to engage in mental processing. Examine the emotion:

- Is it **r**elevant? Take into consideration that emotions are habits, which makes them automatic patterns that can often be irrelevant to the situation at hand.
- Is it **a**ccurate? If your emotion is an automatic pattern, it might be misplaced or exaggerated due to a worn-out perception, belief, assumption, or even an old wound.
- Does it **h**elp with growth? Emotions that do not increase your creativity, inspiration, energy, motivation, and insight hinder your growth.
- What **a**ction does it invoke? How does it help or not? Assess whether the action is getting you closer to or further from your big picture or desired outcome.

Catalysts maintain an equanimous state of composure, groundedness, nonattachment, and mental clarity by developing mastery over their emotions, which empowers them to focus on their big picture in any situation or relationship.

Fixation on the Emotional

A person who is fixated on the Emotional can seem like a walking time bomb and is best avoided. Here are some common signals:

- Emotional overwhelm becomes the determining factor for actions and behaviors
- Inconsistent behavior drains personal and professional relationships
- Inability to navigate difficult conversations effectively
- Struggling with change or focusing efforts in one direction (resistance to change)
- Poor application of learning; stuck in old patterns of thinking, feeling, and behaving
- Dumping uninvited emotional outbursts on people
- Lack of appreciation for others
- Difficulty staying objective or embracing a new perspective
- Addiction to constant stimulation

A good first step for those who spot these patterns in themselves is to pause. Create space between the feeling and your reaction to it. Hold back on reacting long enough for your conscious awareness, or Y2, to kick in and lead the way in processing the physiological reaction, then the mental assessment of emotions.

The Mental (M)

Let's think of your Mental (M) landscape as a garden that needs to be nurtured, cultivated, and maintained. Consider the following:

What is the *landscape* of your garden? How organized is it?

Your mental landscape is the active patterns of your thoughts, beliefs, memories, focus, clarity, and processing. How energizing and enlivening is that landscape for you?

What kind of *plants* are there, if any?

Grass, flowers, vegetables, herbs, fruit-bearing trees, ornamental trees, evergreen trees, or plants that endure harsh weather conditions? Plants represent your ability to learn and perceive. What knowledge do you actively seek? How do you apply it? Is your mental landscape conducive to growth?

How many of these plants are your *choice?*

Are you growing mentally in a direction of your choosing? Or is it happening arbitrarily as life unfolds?

How many *weeds* are there in your garden? How do you control them?

Weeds are thoughts, beliefs, and inner narratives that go unchecked and hinder, or even block, your health, peace, and well-being.

What is your *pest control* (self-preservation) strategy?

How do you shield yourself from negative influences and toxicity?

How much *color* is there in your garden?

How satisfying is it for you to live in your head? What makes it interesting? How do you maintain variety and aliveness?

If you had to *live* in this garden for the rest of your life, how would you feel about that?

Are you comfortable, satisfied, and energized by your mental landscape? What changes would you like to make?

How often do you care for and *maintain* your garden?

How do you keep your mental aspect healthy, balanced, and resilient?

Living in your head can be a haven or a trap. When your mental landscape is your haven, both Y1 (experiencing) and Y2 (witnessing) are active and working together in harmony through your ability to zoom in and out as necessary, keeping sight of the whole (the big picture) and its component parts.

Three factors that affect the health of your Mental (M) aspect are:

1. **What you feed it:** The things you expose it to via watching, listening, and reading, or the stories you allow yourself to believe.
2. **How you use it:** The acuity of your thinking, processing, reasoning, problem-solving, and decision-making.
3. **How you grow it:** Learning and applying the learning to elevate your thinking patterns and behaviors, actively seeking to expand your horizons.

The brain is always active, even during sleep or rest, with varying activity in different areas depending on what you're doing and your physiological and psychological state. The brain's function is affected by how well the Physical and Emotional aspects are cared for and maintained, in addition to how it is stimulated. For example, replaying scenarios and sharing stories that deplete your energy is a dysfunctional stimulation of your Mental aspect, while learning new things or building new habits count as a functional stimulation.

Any thought or inner narrative that does not drive growth, nurturing, clarity, inspiration, energy, motivation, and insight is like a weed or pest. The sooner you rid yourself of it by taking conscious action, letting go, reframing, or distraction, the less likely it is to gain momentum and dominate your mental focus.

The Way of the Catalyst is to care for the Mental aspect like you are caring for a garden, by securing the conditions for it to grow and expand. Catalysts bring unconscious thoughts and inner narratives into conscious awareness, then they tease out what serves the big picture and let go of the rest. They are selective about where they invest their mental energy, which includes what they read, watch, say, listen to, or surround themselves with (more on this in the next topic—The Social Space). They focus on a direction that enhances and elevates their life experience.

Catalysts are often engaged in new learning, such as language, music, sports, dance, theory, skills, or habits. As with the Physical, they find joy in expanding their mental capability. Their processing, reasoning, problem-solving, and decision-making are marked by purposeful choice, with no unnecessary compromises. They balance their own needs, those of others, and situational needs. Some might perceive this way of being as a form of wisdom or long-term thinking.

Fixation on the Mental

Here are some common signals of a person who is fixated on the Mental:

- Overthinking and rumination, leading to exhaustion and inability to see a way out
- Preoccupation with mental stimulation, neglecting the Physical, Emotional, and Social aspects
- Obsession with hoarding knowledge, with little to no application or use of learning
- Dismissive of anything that does not make sense to them
- Mental arrogance—coming across as superior to others
- Communicating with jargon and complex language
- A cynical and critical attitude that alienates people and diminishes trust
- Judging others by what they know

The Mental aspect is compromised when the character is not developed well enough to use their mental capacity to serve themselves and the world around them effectively.

The Social Space (S)

The Social Space is everything external to you: the family you come from, the family you create or choose, your extended family, romantic partners or spouses, in-laws, work colleagues, supervisors, clients, friends, neighbors, community, school teachers, classmates, peers, digital contacts (people you follow and those who follow you on social media), people connected with you through shared activities like sports or hobbies, mentors, therapists, professional guides, casual acquaintances, and so on.

You are constantly and consistently making an impact on your Social Space, and it is impacting you in return. It holds up a mirror reflecting what's going on within you. For example, when your thoughts and emotions embody low self-esteem, you'll find yourself surrounded by people who are judgmental and critical. When your inner world is driven by fear, you'll find threats all around. When you're motivated by guilt, the Social Space will be filled with those who blame and criticize you. When you are angry with life, it becomes a series of frustrating and annoying events. When you emanate love, power, and appreciation, people around you will be supportive and nurturing, and they will be energized and fulfilled through their interactions with you.

The Social Space is a prime communicator of calls for change. It presents challenges that prompt your growth and expansion, learnings for you to leverage, and insights that lead to a deeper understanding of yourself, others, life, and the world around you.

Like a physical space, the Social Space needs to be cleaned up, organized or reorganized, maintained, and nurtured on an ongoing basis. Your time and energy are limited, and you are probably investing the bulk of them in the Social Space. Life experience thrives when the Social Space is supportive, nurturing, truthful, and safe (physically and psychologically).

The Social Space is governed by observed natural social laws that operate as core concepts shaping interactions and outcomes. These laws are universal and independent of the human-made justice system, laws, or institutions. Understanding these invisible guidelines allows for a harmonious social fabric, balanced interactions, and graceful living.

Let's explore four of those laws:

1. **Necessity of social life:** No one possesses all capabilities, talents, or skills. We survive and progress through our collaborations and interactions with others.
2. **Reciprocity:** You receive back in multiple what you give, whether positive or negative, though not necessarily through the same channels. This process isn't always immediate, but it's consistently at work.

3. **Justice:** Each person carries an innate sense of what is fair and just, a moral compass that exists independently of human-made laws or legislation.

4. **Mid-point:** We are positioned between those who guide and support us and those whom we guide and support. This dynamic is independent of financial responsibilities or transactions.

The Way of the Catalyst is to engage the Social Space with integrity, respect, appreciation, and understanding. Catalysts fulfill their role(s), taking these natural social laws into account. They establish a clear code of social conduct for themselves that makes them predictable, consistent, and trustworthy. Because of this, others find it easy and comfortable to engage with them, and they build strong, meaningful connections with the world around them.

Fixation on the Social Space

Here are some common signals of a person who is fixated on the Social Space:

- Overindulgence in social stimulation, avoiding sitting with oneself
- Wide circle of superficial social contacts in which nobody is nurtured or nurturing
- Addiction to social media

- Fascination with gossip and tale-telling
- Obsession with personal image and how it is perceived by others
- Constant busyness that leaves no room for rest, reflection, or contemplation
- Disconnection from the body and emotions, and a lack of awareness of inner narratives
- Reacting without taking any responsibility for the impact
- Addiction to noise and drama

In general, when the Social Space is random, excessive, and erratic, it can function as a vacuum for your time and energy in meaningless and sometimes harmful ways, and it can bring drama into your life.

Stephen Karpman, a renowned psychiatrist, psychologist, and teacher of Transaction Analysis, developed the Drama Triangle as a model for social interaction.[9] It's an inverted triangle that points out three dysfunctional roles of victimhood:

1. Victim—convinced of being powerless, helpless, and hopeless
2. Persecutor—blaming others and justifying attacking them as self-protection
3. Rescuer—"saving others" and fostering dependency and toxic dynamics

The common factor in all three roles is a refusal to take responsibility. Victims refuse to take responsibility for themselves, persecutors for their actions, and rescuers for their needs. It is called the Drama Triangle because once you are in the triangle, the outcome is always drama. Nobody wins. The only way to take control of your life is by stepping out of the drama and taking responsibility for yourself (your needs, actions, and impact).

The Big Picture Personal Canvas enables you to keep the basic aspects of your being contained. It is not a vague dream for the future; it is alive in the here-and-now reality of your PEMS dimensions. The simple truth is that your time and energy are limited, your health is conditional, and you are vulnerable to your environment. It is crucial to intentionally design your big picture in a way that's meaningful to you, and to do so with a sense of urgency.

The Big Picture Personal Canvas framework

The Big Picture Personal Canvas framework helps you design your own big picture to sustain and replenish your PEMS aspects. The framework consists of the following seven questions:

1. What is my desired outcome?

2. What are the measurable elements (how will I know I'm achieving it)?
3. What do I need to start from scratch (something new that I've never done before)?
4. What do I need to keep the same?
5. What needs some change (to make it more effective)?
6. What needs to go (what must I stop doing)?
7. When shall I action all of these by (my timeline)?

Below is my Big Picture Personal Canvas as an example (this reflects where I was at the time I wrote this book). Of course, it is not fixed, but rather dynamic and constantly evolving over time. The answers to questions 2–7 often shift, depending on your focus or priorities at any given period.

1. What is my desired outcome?	
Physical	• Increase strength, balance, and mobility while preserving joint health, muscle tone, and cardiovascular fitness for long-term vitality and ease of movement.
Emotional	• Enhance emotional mastery by growing inner peace and feeling light and carefree. • Continue to find joy in the small things and live every moment with presence, awareness, and appreciation.

Mental

- Stimulate my mind with new learning and cultivate energizing thoughts that bring clarity, creativity, and a sense of expansion and forward momentum.

Social

- Be a catalyst for clarity, fulfillment, and aliveness in those I support and care for.
- Nurture meaningful relationships that are rooted in honesty, presence, and shared joy.

---

2. How will I know it's happening (measurable elements)?

Physical

- Dancing the Argentinian tango like a pro, which requires strength, balance, and flexibility.
- Jogging for twenty minutes with controlled breathing.
- Doing a 30-mile bike ride in one go.

Emotional

- Recovering from a spike of negative emotions in less than two minutes.
- Managing hormonal fluctuations with a healthy diet, necessary supplements, consistent workouts, and sufficient sleep.
- Curating a "pick-me-up kit" for an instant energy boost. This includes movement, music, meaningful content, and creative inspiration.
- Living a lifestyle that steadily stabilizes and renews my energy.

Mental

- Engaging in deep learning on one subject at a time.
- At high-pressure times, pausing for a few moments to gain clarity before responding in creative and meaningful ways.
- Catching unhelpful thoughts within ten seconds, before they gain momentum, and consciously choosing an inner narrative that supports growth, clarity, and alignment.

Social	• Enlivening interactions with clients, family, and friends every day. • Embracing feedback, whether direct or subtle, at least five times a month. • Spending quality time with my best friend at least once a week. • Contacting my parents once a week and spending the holiday season with them. Being fully present and eliminating all distractions. Investing time in getting to know them on a deeper level. • Helping clients set clear goals for our coaching engagement and measuring their progress. • Getting together with my small social circles at least once every three months.

3. What do I need to start from scratch (something new that I've never done before)?	
Physical	• Jogging twice a week. • Learning how to ride a bike.
Emotional	• Doing acupuncture therapy. • Learning how different foods impact emotional health.
Mental	• Studying Transactional Analysis in depth.
Social	• Taking at least two weeks off over Christmas and New Year, and during summer.

4. What do I need to keep the same?	
Physical	• Doing yoga, deep stretching, mobility training, and Argentinian tango classes, each twice weekly.

Emotional
- Observing emotions, harnessing their message, and fine-tuning my inner narrative.
- Pausing to appreciate the little things.
- Celebrating deep, meaningful connections.

Mental
- Cultivating curiosity about the human psyche.
- Playing word and number games.

Social
- Being present and fully engaged in my interactions and relationships.
- Being committed to the job and to the role I play in others' journeys.

---

5. What needs some change (to minimize wasted effort and make it more effective)?

Physical
- Avoiding sitting for long periods by introducing intervals of standing, moving around, or taking short walks throughout the workday.

Emotional
- Adjusting my schedule to include moments of stillness and nothingness.

Mental
- Avoiding getting side-tracked by exploring rabbit holes that pull me away from the main topic of my study.

Social
- Ensuring I attend social gatherings that I care about rather than missing out.

---

6. What needs to go (what must I stop doing)?

Physical
- Late nights working or studying, leading to fewer hours of sleep.

Emotional
- Fast-paced routine packed with activities, tasks, and responsibilities.

Mental
- Signing up for more than one course at a time as it compromises the depth of my learning.

Social	• Being part of group chats that I no longer want to engage with. • Maintaining relationships that I no longer resonate with.
7. When shall I action all of these by (my timeline)?	
Physical	• Starting today and ongoing.
Emotional	• By the end of the calendar year.
Mental	• By the beginning of the academic year.
Social	• Starting now and ongoing.

Key points

- The Big Picture Personal Canvas consists of your Physical (P), Emotional (E), Mental (M), and Social Space (S) (PEMS) dimensions.
- The main focus areas for the health of the Physical aspect are:
  - Nutrition and hydration
  - Rest and repair
  - Tenacity (stamina, endurance, strength)
  - Flexibility (of joints, muscles, and spine)
  - State of vital and endocrine systems
- The Emotional (E) aspect links the Physical (P) and the Mental (M). Processing emotions requires you to attend to both endpoints, P and M.

- The main focus areas for the health of the Mental (M) aspect are:
  - What you feed it.
  - How you use it.
  - How you grow it.
- The Social Space (S) involves everything external to you, such as the people you interact with and impact, and who impact you in return.
- The Big Picture Personal Canvas is not a vague dream for the future—it is alive in the here and now, dynamic and constantly evolving over time.

PART TWO

FIVE ATTITUDES OF THE CATALYST

Attitudes are often passed down and end up shaping the culture of families, communities, and organizations. Breaking the cycle of a toxic, dysfunctional cascade starts with you. You, the Catalyst, blaze a path into a future that transcends the past and even the present.

In his book, *See You At The Top*, Zig Ziglar, a legendary motivational speaker and author, said:

> "And because your attitude is so important,
> and because it affects so many other people,
> and because it is catching, we want to always
> remember that, as we explore our attitudes,
> we ask ourselves the question, 'Is my attitude

> worth catching? Or if anybody does catch it, will they be worse off as a result of it?'"[10]

Then he told a powerful story about the impact of attitudes. The story of Mr. B, the leader of a successful company, who gave an inspiring speech to his team about discipline, commitment, and the effective use of time. Mr. B promised to lead by example by going the extra mile, staying longer at the office, minimizing distractions, and focusing only on work during working hours.

However, about three weeks later, Mr. B lost track of time at a business chat over lunch at the country club. He rushed back to the office, only to get a speeding ticket. Furious, he took his frustration out at work. He called his sales manager, and everybody could hear Mr. B scolding and threatening to fire him for losing a major client. Feeling upset, the sales manager turned and snapped at his secretary, blaming her for delays in sending some letters and threatening to fire her. The secretary, in turn, lashed out at the switchboard operator, dumping extra work on her and threatening to fire her if she didn't get the job done immediately.

The operator got the job done, but she was still feeling furious when she reached home. When she saw her son lying on the carpet watching television, still in his school trousers rather than his play clothes, she punished him by sending him to his room without dinner and banning television for the next three weeks. The young boy, feeling frustrated and mistreated, went to his room and kicked his cat.

Ziglar humorously pointed out, "Wouldn't it have been much better if Mr. B had just gone directly from the country club to that switchboard operator's house and kicked that cat himself, and left all of those other people out of it?"

Attitudes are contagious. Scientific research on mirror neurons and emotional contagion shows that we unconsciously absorb the moods and energies of those with whom we interact. Consciously choosing your attitude is an expression of personal power that can influence the attitudes of others, shaping the collective experience in subtle yet powerful ways.

In Part Two, you will explore the Five Attitudes of the Catalyst:

1. **Responsibility (R):** Taking charge of inner thoughts, emotions, and stories.
2. **Proactivity (P):** Living life by design.
3. **Interdependence (I):** Sharing power with all involved.
4. **Influence (F):** Causing an effect without force.
5. **Excellence (X):** Bringing the dynamic self, moment to moment.

Each attitude is lived and experienced through three traits (R1, R2, R3, etc.). There are five proficiency levels for every attitude and its traits. Each proficiency level reflects the dynamic interplay between awareness, action or application, and impact.

The proficiency levels are marked by:

1. **Level 1:** Lack of awareness ("I don't know, and I don't know that I don't know.").
2. **Level 2:** Some awareness, but no action ("I have an idea, but there's nothing I can do about it.").
3. **Level 3:** Awareness with some acting upon it ("I know, and I try sometimes.").
4. **Level 4:** Awareness and application most of the time ("I know what needs to be done, and I do it. I'm intentional about continuously growing and expanding myself, and I have a powerful impact on my surroundings.").
5. **Level 5:** Alignment in thought, speech, and action; consistency in generating an intentional ripple effect that impacts the environment in resourceful and creative ways ("My attitudes and behaviors reflect clarity and integrity. The outcomes I seek and achieve are harmonious and aligned with the greater good and collective progress.").

The following five chapters will guide you through achieving proficiency level 5 thoughts and behavior patterns for each attitude and its traits. Only proficiency level 5 is presented. Similarly to when you learn a dance or a sport, the training starts by showing you the expert level of each move and step, and you're held to that standard to help you grow into mastery.

Read, integrate, transform, and enjoy.

3

Responsibility: Taking Charge Of Inner Thoughts, Emotions, And Stories

Your inner narrative is the story you tell yourself about yourself, others, and how the world works. It consists of your thoughts, beliefs, interpretations, and emotional associations. It often runs beneath the surface of your conscious awareness.

The choices you make, your decisions, and the stands you take are all products of your inner narrative and the set of thoughts and emotions that come with it. Consciously or unconsciously, you reinforce them every time you repeat the same story, whether in your head or out loud to someone else. Your inner narrative, then, shapes your quality of life and determines how you show up, how you relate, and the difference you make.

The direction of your inner narrative is binary. It's either moving you forward or keeping you stuck in the status quo. Life constantly presents you with opportunities for growth, evolution, and expansion, often by challenging old thought patterns and emotions that stand in the way of your progress. A narrative that's resistant to growth blocks your ability to manage yourself effectively and to redirect your course when it matters the most. During difficult situations, it becomes essential to align your inner narrative with the solution (being future-focused), rather than the problem (being past-focused). This alignment allows you to access the clarity, strength, and freedom necessary to make effective choices and take timely actions.

In his book, *Stumbling On Happiness*, Daniel Gilbert, a social psychologist, Harvard professor, and bestselling author, explains that, "memories, especially memories of experiences, are notoriously unreliable."[11] He shared findings of a study in which researchers showed volunteers a color swatch and allowed them to study it for five seconds. Some volunteers then spent thirty seconds describing the color, while other volunteers did not. All volunteers were then shown a lineup of six color swatches, one of which was the color that they had seen thirty seconds earlier, and were asked to pick out the original swatch. The findings were as follows:

- 73% of the volunteers who did not describe the color were able to identify it accurately.

- Only 33% of the volunteers who described the color were able to accurately identify the correct swatch.

The results indicated that describing the color impaired, rather than improved, their performance on the identification task. According to Gilbert, "the volunteers' verbal descriptions overwrote their memories of the experiences themselves, and they ended up remembering not what they had experienced, but what they had said about what they experienced."

The story you tell yourself matters. In fact, it often matters more than what actually happened, because that story is going to stay with you and impact you longer than the actual event. Stories are a powerful tool to make meaning and generate emotions. Their impact has a life-changing effect. When an inner narrative escapes your conscious awareness and continues uninterrupted, it snowballs, gaining momentum the more you think about it or share it with others.

Living from the inside out

Your life story is a collage of everyday encounters, relationships, and experiences. Hardly any of those stories is 100% accurate. If they were, then others who shared those stories with you would see them in exactly the same way, which is not usually the case. Why is that? Because at any point in time, full information is not available to any one person. So, when an event takes place, you unconsciously complete the missing pieces with what you already know, with what's familiar. This is a problem because when more information becomes available, it is too late to take it in or consider it. The story seems complete, leaving no room for anything new, even the truth. Where does that lead? Likely to chaos, confusion, and conflict.

During my foundation year in Transactional Analysis (TA) at The Berne Institute, I had the privilege of learning from Adrienne Lee, a world-class teacher, trainer, and co-founder of the institute, whose contributions to the field of TA are significant and far-reaching.

On one of the training days, Adrienne said, "What we have to do is tolerate the discomfort long enough for our conscious mind to kick in and say, 'Hello, hello, hello! What's going on here? What is this about?' rather than to go quickly into saying, 'I know what this is about.'"

Adrienne's insight points to a powerful moment—the moment between an event taking place and us assigning meaning to it—when responsibility truly begins. When you acknowledge that your stories may not be entirely accurate, you create space to pause, seek clarity, and remain open to new information, trusting your ability to integrate it.

That pause, when you get curious and expand your perception of any situation, often takes a few minutes, but sometimes only seconds. And the truth is, most situations can wait at least that long. Giving yourself even a brief moment to reflect before reacting can make the difference between being an emotional disaster and an emotional master.

A few years ago, I took a road trip through Portugal with my best friend. One morning, while walking around the beautiful city of Coimbra, we noticed a historic building on top of a hill overlooking the city. It was Coimbra prison. I said, "The view must be amazing from up there."

She replied, "Yes, and they're giving that wonderful view to the prisoners." That simple observation sparked a conversation about how prisoners are treated and whether the system truly prepares them for reintegration into society. We had opposing views, and the conversation quickly escalated into a heated debate.

Looking back, I remember how caught up I was in the argument. In the heat of the moment, I completely lost sight of the bigger question: "Why am I even engaging in this debate?" In reality, it didn't matter that we disagreed. We simply saw things differently, and that was OK. In that unguarded moment, I turned away from the big picture. Instead of regulating what stirred inside me, I became fixated on what my friend said and how she said it. That shift in focus, from internal awareness to external control, was a mistake. We both became reactive, and the argument spiraled out of control. Eventually, we stopped talking altogether and avoided each other for the rest of the day.

In that situation, I didn't give myself the space to pause and reflect on the purpose of the interaction. I was so zoomed in on our differing viewpoints that I lost sight of the true purpose of the trip: to relax and have fun. The rest of the day felt tense, and honestly, it wasn't worth it.

Years later, we still laugh about it. Our views haven't changed, but we've both grown wiser and more able to quickly catch ourselves and let go of the need to change each other's perspectives. Our friendship has only grown deeper and stronger as we've learned to better accept our differences

The life lesson I took from that experience was invaluable: chasing the illusion of external control blocks inner freedom. The moment I tried to control my friend's perspective, wanting to prove a point and win the debate, I lost the ability to pause, zoom out, and reconnect with the big picture. In being reactive, I gave away my freedom to choose—to disengage from what doesn't matter and stay connected to what truly does.

You have probably heard the saying, "With freedom comes responsibility." When freedom is exercised without responsibility, it can lead to chaos. Think of an adult throwing a tantrum, expressing their frustration freely, but without any self-regulation or accountability for their personal impact. This kind of behavior can cause real damage, sometimes irreversible, in both personal and professional relationships.

The reverse of that famous saying is also true: "With responsibility comes freedom." That freedom only emerges when responsibility is directed inward as well as outward—not just toward your job, family, or community, but also toward your inner thoughts, feelings, and stories. When responsibility is limited to external roles, it may look admirable on the outside but often feels heavy and restrictive on the inside. Why? Because in that state, you're at the mercy of external triggers, reacting on autopilot, without the freedom to consciously choose your responses.

True responsibility begins within, by taking ownership of your thoughts, emotions, and inner narratives. That's where your inner freedom lives.

When the path is unclear and the pressure is high, actively filtering your thoughts and processing your emotions, moving beyond them, and choosing a narrative that aligns with your big picture creates an inner strength that no one can take from you. You begin to trust that there is light at the end of the tunnel, even when you can't see it.

A wise man once told me, "The ultimate purpose in life is to close the gap between who you are now and who you are becoming." Life gains a new momentum when you begin to rewrite the inner stories you hold about the past, the present, who you are, what you're capable of, and the world around you. One story at a time, just when life calls for it. With each update, you close the gap between who you are and who you are becoming, aligning more fully with your future, expanded self.

The Way of the Catalyst is to bring the inner story into conscious awareness and examine the truth and effectiveness of what you're telling yourself. It means turning dead-end statements into questions that open the space for exploration and discovery. It's about taking responsibility for what is brewing within, reframing it to reclaim your ability to effect meaningful change in alignment with your big picture, and holding focus on an enlivening perspective that moves you toward growth and advancement.

Three traits of Responsibility

Responsibility is the first attitude of the Catalyst and is expressed through three interwoven traits:

- R1: Awareness of emotional states and their impact
- R2: Mastery in selecting emotions for effectiveness
- R3: Making a life-affirming choice every time

You often experience a dominant set of emotions that leads to repeated, predictable outcomes. Taking responsibility for your inner world means being able to zoom out in the heat of the moment, recognize where a particular emotional state is leading you, and consciously choose to pause, regulate the emotion, and select a narrative that aligns with outcomes that reflect your Big Picture Personal Canvas (refer to Chapter Two).

A life-affirming choice is a choice that is:

- Derived from the big picture—reflecting your principles and long-term direction
- Repeatable—intentional, grounded, and sustainable over time
- Measurable—with observable impact, whether tangible or intangible
- Active—generating movement toward growth and meaningful progress

This lays the foundation for you to expand into who you are becoming. Choosing your thoughts and feelings is an expression of your free will, and you are gifted with the capacity and the mechanism to do so.

Rational lies: Logic as a disguise

The most effective way to shift how you feel is to become aware of the thought behind the feeling and choose a better one. After all, not every thought is rooted in truth. Sometimes, what appears to be a logical thought is actually fear disguised as reason. Rationalizations and justifications often act as defense mechanisms—ways in which you protect yourself from the discomfort of the situation, avoid taking personal responsibility, or resist the call for change. They come in the shape of:

- **Discounting:** Failing to recognize a problem, its significance, change possibilities, or your personal abilities.[12] It's like making a molehill out of a mountain. Discounting is when your thoughts and feelings about a situation are more important than the situation itself. In other words, reality becomes distorted by your perception—the lens through which you see your life, others, and the world. An example of this is when you are facing a problem, and you're in denial, thinking:
  - "That's not a big deal. Some people dream of being in my place." (Discounting the problem.)
  - "Life goes on, it will pass." (Discounting the problem's significance.)
  - "There's nothing I can do about it." (Discounting change possibilities.)
  - "I can never get it done, and I don't know what to do anyway." (Discounting personal ability.)

- **Grandiosity:** A purposeful exaggeration or distortion of reality about the self, others, or situations to justify feelings of inadequacy. This is when you suggest that something or someone else is responsible for your feelings and behaviors.[13] It's like making a mountain out of a molehill. Here are examples of what you might hear yourself saying if you hide behind grandiosity:
  - "I can't stand it."
  - "I got so mad that I lost control."
  - "I'm *always*..."
  - "I can *never*..."
  - "It's not my fault."
  - "That's just the way I am."
  - "I have no choice."

When you exaggerate an aspect of reality, you usually discount another. In both cases, there's a disconnect with reality and a preoccupation with the subjective inner experience, sometimes to the exclusion of the objective, outer reality. This dynamic keeps you in a comfort zone that protects you from the discomfort of taking responsibility for your inner narrative and actively participating in solving a problem or initiating change.

However, comfort zones are not truly comfortable; they're simply familiar. Usually, obstacles, challenges, and even dreams call for you to step outside of your comfort zone. The calling often increases in intensity until you answer it.

One of your most powerful abilities is the capacity to observe your thoughts, emotions, and stories from a state of being unattached, creating a space between you and your thoughts, and allowing you to clearly appraise and intentionally choose a narrative that enlivens you to move through life with energy, grace, and meaning.

Your reality starts to shift when you "rewrite" the story you're telling yourself. You are then leading change from within by taking responsibility for your inner world, creating an intentional ripple effect that elevates your life and your surroundings

---

CASE STUDY: The truth beneath the surface

Ms. D is a fierce lawyer, known for her powerful presence, persuasive arguments, and dedication to the job. She was promised a promotion to partner, but when the news finally came, it wasn't what she expected. The promotion hadn't gone through.

She went home that evening, simmering with frustration, thinking, "This job has been my priority for twelve years, and this is what I get? Thankless disregard? That's outrageous!" The more she replayed the situation in her head, the more her disappointment snowballed into anger and resentment.

The next morning, she woke with a dull headache. Instead of spiraling further, she got up, laced her shoes, and took a walk in the park nearby. It was Saturday morning, and the park was buzzing with children running around laughing, dogs chasing balls, and people lying in the sunshine. Something in the simplicity of that scene helped her settle down.

As she walked, she began to reflect. The sting of disappointment was still present, but now she was asking real questions: "How could they have passed me over? What am I not seeing? I need to understand this before I decide what to do next."

By Monday morning, she was ready. She scheduled a meeting with the managing partner. Calm and composed, she said, "My experience at this firm has always been one of fairness and integrity. I'm assuming something must have gotten in the way of my promotion. I'd really appreciate some clarity on what happened."

The managing partner paused, then said, "I appreciate your directness, D. The truth is, we're preparing to announce a merger. All senior promotions have been temporarily paused until the new structure is finalized. Please hang in there. Your contribution is essential, and we value your work and commitment."

Ms. D took in the response, sat with it, and decided to continue her work with her usual enthusiasm and determination. Two years later, she was named partner, with the option to buy equity in the firm.

You might think Ms. D was fortunate to work for a company that recognized her effort and rewarded her accordingly. You might even say, "That's not often the case; many people work hard and still aren't treated fairly or professionally." And you'd be right. Here's what's worth remembering: taking charge of your inner thoughts, emotions, and stories empowers you to gain clarity, build strength, and free yourself from emotional hijacking, so you can recognize your options and respond with intent.

It expands your capacity to influence outcomes, especially in challenging situations. When Ms. D received the news that she had been passed over for promotion, she felt angry, betrayed, and resentful. That emotional storm lasted all day, and understandably so. It's natural to feel this way. Some people might have justified lashing out or walking away on the spot (grandiosity). She could have chosen to meet the managing partner in that state and had the conversation right there and then. But she knew that her emotions were running high, and that it was not the right time to have a conversation (she was aware of her emotional states and their impact).

She woke up the next morning still unsettled. What did she do? She went for a walk. Moving her body and getting some fresh air and sunlight were simple actions that helped her think and separate her assumption ("They're a thankless bunch who can't be trusted!") from reality ("I don't know why I didn't get the promotion; I need to find out."). That intentional shift from emotional reaction to curious inquiry was a good demonstration of R2, the second trait of Responsibility (mastery in selecting emotions for effectiveness).

When she met with the managing partner, her words were clear and respectful, without a shred of blame, criticism, or victimhood. Her only goal was to understand what had happened. Asking in the way she did was a life-affirming choice that not only fulfilled the purpose of the conversation (to get clarity) but also secured her professional reputation and identity. Had the decision truly been unfair on the part of the firm's leadership, Ms. D was wise enough to approach the situation without burning bridges or causing offense (making a life-affirming choice every time). Her composure allowed the managing partner to meet her with equal clarity and respect.

Let's examine Ms. D's attitude from another perspective, looking at what she chose not to do. She did not:

- React impulsively or lose control, which she may have felt was justified, given her shock
- Ignore how she felt or what she needed to clear her head
- Stay stuck on the initial narrative
- Do nothing about it

- Rush into a decision or conclusion, dismissing the simple act of asking to understand
- Discount her options for handling the situation
- Make a life-diminishing choice of passivity, aggression, over-expressing, or power play

The three traits of Responsibility—awareness of emotional states and their impact, mastery in selecting emotions for effectiveness, and making a life-affirming choice every time—are deeply interlinked. Awareness is the foundation of emotional mastery, and in turn, it empowers you to choose responses that align with your big picture.

These intentional choices shape outcomes and build success across all areas of life—careers, businesses, relationships, health and well-being, and the social space at large.

Responsibility: Proficiency level 5

What it usually sounds like:

- I am consistently positive in what I think, say, and do, and these three things are aligned.
- I am aware of how what I say and do impacts the world around me, and I focus on being effective in my speech and actions. No word is out of place, and there's no action that I regret.

- People ask me for help with being calm and managing their emotions, and I am happy to share tips that worked for me.
- I am aware of my emotions and feelings, but they don't solely determine or influence the way I perceive situations.
- In difficult situations, I am able to first manage myself (emotions and self-talk) before I attempt to manage the situation.
- I know that I always have a choice and can control the way I feel about something.
- I am able to choose my tone, emotions, words, and actions to benefit myself and the people around me.
- I examine the facts.
- I look at all options and all forms of resources.
- I examine why we think this is the way forward.

R1: Awareness of emotional states and their impact

The consistent ability to observe what story, narrative, self-talk, emotional state, or rationalization is being invoked in that moment, from a state of unattached observation that aligns with the Big Picture Personal Canvas that one desires for oneself.

What it usually sounds like:

- I would rather ask questions to first better understand what is happening than jump to conclusions based on my past experiences or let my feelings and emotions get the better of me.
- During difficult times, I can shift my and others' attention and focus to what is relevant and really important.
- I accept my feelings without the need to discount or exaggerate them. I process and shift with ease and grace.
- I can remain calm when people around me are losing theirs.
- In situations that matter, I am able to quickly distinguish facts from feelings and select what helps me remain effective. I help others do this, too.
- I eliminate habits that no longer serve their purpose.
- I welcome change and challenges, as they give me a chance to know myself better and work on improving myself.
- I carry an air of happiness, peace, positivity, and hope.

R2: Mastery in selecting emotions for effectiveness

The consistent ability to determine an effective outcome for a situation that is aligned with the Big Picture Personal Canvas, and then to select a story, narrative, interpretation, or emotional state that supports that choice, and radiate that on the outside.

What it usually sounds like:

- I give myself a moment to compose myself before I say or do anything.
- In difficult situations with others, I approach conversations with love, compassion, and assertiveness. This helps me get through.
- I can regulate my feelings so as not to hinder progress or affect my performance negatively.
- I am able to minimize negativity without underestimating its relevance, while focusing on the big picture and what is positive in myself and others.
- I can stay composed during the best and worst of times. For me, to be human is to have the choice to master myself.
- I can sense what people are feeling even when they don't say it and can adjust myself to be effective.

R3: Making a life-affirming choice every time

The consistent ability to consciously make a choice, from all the perceived available options, that aligns with the Big Picture Personal Canvas that one desires for oneself, and radiate that on the outside.

What it usually sounds like:

- I know that, ultimately, even if I don't have control over a situation, I can decide how I respond to it, despite how it appears or what it may feel like.
- Before I do anything, in the moment, I am able to quickly ask myself what the big picture is and then manage myself first, before anything else.
- I study, reflect on, and determine how my actions, thoughts, and feelings contribute to the situation, and I am able to rise above it.
- I think, "Win-win or no deal."
- Yes, there was a setback. It doesn't have to affect everything.
- If it didn't go as planned, I take responsibility for my actions. I move forward and attempt again, using what I've learned. There is no point in blaming others or circumstances.
- Life is incredible if we participate in it.
- There is always a choice, even if it is not evident.

- My choices are linked to a bigger picture I have for myself. Each day can be a smaller version of the life I want to lead.
- I am patient with myself and others when we navigate unfamiliar situations using familiar methods.

Key points

- Responsibility: Taking charge of inner thoughts, emotions, and stories:
  - R1: Awareness of emotional states and their impact.
  - R2: Mastery in selecting emotions for effectiveness.
  - R3: Making a life-affirming choice every time.
- The direction of your inner narrative is binary. It's either moving you forward or keeping you stuck in the status quo.
- The story you tell yourself matters more than what actually happened, because that story is going to stay with you and impact you longer than the actual event.
- External control is an illusion. You cannot control others' thoughts or feelings; you can only influence them.

- Choosing your thoughts and feelings is an expression of your free will, and you are gifted with the capacity and the mechanism to do so.
- Rationalizations and justifications are defense mechanisms—ways you protect yourself from the discomfort of the situation, avoid taking personal responsibility, or resist the call for change.
- When you exaggerate an aspect of reality, you usually discount another. In both cases, there's a disconnect with reality and a preoccupation with the subjective inner experience, sometimes to the exclusion of the objective outer reality.
- Your reality starts to shift when you "rewrite" the story you're telling yourself.
- Taking charge of your inner thoughts, emotions, and stories empowers you to gain clarity, build strength, and free yourself from emotional hijacking, so you can recognize your options and respond intentionally.
- Awareness is the foundation of emotional mastery, and in turn, it empowers you to choose responses that align with your big picture.

4

Proactivity: Living Life By Design

The second attitude of the Catalyst, Proactivity, is an expansion of inner responsibility into action. Proactivity sets the inner narrative into motion; it's the outward expression of what you choose to do with your sense of agency. It means getting ahead of everyday life with clear intention and living by your own design in alignment with your Big Picture Personal Canvas.

The power and freedom granted to us in adult life are sometimes overlooked or underused. Your Integrated Time Awareness (ITA) (see Chapter One) unlocks your ability to live by design as a grown-up. ITA is the practice of fully engaging in the present moment, grounded in wisdom drawn from past experiences, and leveraging inner and outer resources to shape an elevated reality guided by an intentional big picture.

Often, we run our lives from a past perspective, which is why proactivity became a thing; it's rare.

Living life by design begins with an honest appraisal of your current reality and your role in shaping it. Whether that reality needs to be refined, redefined, or completely transformed, the shift from reactivity to creativity happens through making a consistent and conscious effort until the new pattern becomes second nature. It's a simple shift in theory, much like moving the "c" in "reactive" to the beginning of the word to spell "creative." But simple doesn't mean easy, especially when it comes to changing attitudes, behaviors, or thought patterns. Inner resilience and grit are required to stay the course. Over time, your reactions are no longer a threat to your life or relationships, because the new replaces the old and becomes your default. You begin to live in harmony with your Big Picture Personal Canvas.

Three traits of proactivity

Proactivity is expressed through these three interwoven traits:

- P1: Recognizing one's own role in creating possibilities
- P2: Taking action by conscious choice
- P3: Demonstrating inner resilience

For the catalyst way of living, Proactivity is measured by these three components. It begins with creating possibilities, seeing beyond the immediate reality, and imagining what could be. Next comes the conscious choice to act, selecting a course that aligns with your big picture. Finally, it requires inner strength to withstand the consequences of that action, whether expected or not, with resilience and responsibility. Together, these three elements allow us to live life by design.

Life as a lump of clay

Think of life as a lump of clay handed to you at birth. Initially, it is shaped by your parents or parental figures, and then shaped further by your wider social space. As you reach adulthood, you continue to sculpt it, using mature intellectual reasoning and free will.

In my third year of university, I met Mr. E, my friend's dad. He was passionate about making horses out of clay. He turned a small room at his house into a workstation. It was filled with natural light and had a rectangular table in the center covered with sculpting tools, clay, and carving materials. The shelves against the wall were filled with sculptures of various sizes. One day, my friend and I dropped by while he was working. It was my first time seeing a sculpting workshop. He said, "Setting your space well helps you focus and enjoy your work. You envision your structure, then sketch it on paper. From there, it is a matter of knowing what tools to use, when, and how. Start with the basic form, then move to the details."

Mr. E's description of his sculpting process captures the essence of Proactivity's three traits and the practical application of each:

- **Setting the space:** Creating a mental space to help you focus and enjoy the process. For P1 (recognizing one's own role in creating possibilities), this means repurposing your energy, reorganizing your priorities, reallocating your time, and filtering your relationships, thoughts, and activities, with a focus on keeping only what matters, to allow new possibilities to unfold.
- **Envisioning the outcome:** This helps generate purposeful actions aligned with the big picture. In P2 (taking conscious action), you ask yourself the questions, "Why am I doing this? What is the outcome I am seeking? What specific action will bring about my desired outcome?" If you've lost sight of what you're doing and why, pause, reset, and then resume.
- **Using your tools:** P3 (inner resilience) comes from actively developing and drawing on a set of life tools that support your physical, emotional, mental, and social well-being. The more prepared and reliable your personal toolbox is, the better able you are to stay grounded under pressure.

> The best time to learn life skills is before you need them, when there's calm and relative stability.

Like carving a sculpture, shaping your life experience requires space to create possibilities, a clear vision to guide your deliberate action, and the effective use of inner tools to stay resilient.

Next, we will explore an example that is a fine demonstration of steady leadership and the Five Attitudes of the Catalyst at the highest level.

Miracle on the Hudson

In a 2019 interview, Captain Chesley Burnett Sullenberger, known as "Sully," recounts the critical moments of the US Airways flight 1549 emergency landing on the Hudson River on January 15, 2009.[14] The flight took off from New York City's LaGuardia Airport, only to be struck two minutes later by a flock of birds, leading to the loss of all engine power at an altitude of approximately 2,800 feet, or 850 meters. Sully began the interview by saying, "January 15, 2009, started just like 10,000 other days, literally." He continued, "But this very suddenly became the worst day of my life."

Realizing the engines had completely failed midair, Sully and his co-pilot, Jeffrey Skiles, had to think of a solution and execute it in under three and a half minutes. Pilots have three key priorities in a time of crisis: to save human life, to save the aircraft if possible, and to minimize ground impact by avoiding densely populated areas and critical infrastructure while executing an emergency landing.

The air traffic controller, Patrick Harten, was guiding Sully toward a possible emergency landing at an airport. The first option was to go back to LaGuardia. The second was landing at Teterboro Airport in New Jersey, across the Hudson. Sully recognized both were unreachable. He told the controller, "We're going to be in the Hudson."

At that time, only military pilots were trained to land on water. Commercial airline pilots were not required to, although cabin crew would demonstrate a pre-flight safety briefing to passengers on evacuating an aircraft in water. In pilot training, it was not possible to practice water landings because flight simulators were not programmed for it. Fortunately, Sully had prior experience as a US Air Force pilot, where he had learned emergency procedures beyond civil training.

Sully, with his extensive experience and strong discipline, focused on his highest priorities, eliminating all distractions. He chose to do only what was necessary to save the 155 lives on board while minimizing damage to the aircraft and to the city's infrastructure.

Under crushing time pressure and the intensity of managing a crisis in which every second counted for survival, Sully had to weigh the available options, create a possibility where none seemed to exist, make a decision, and follow through with confidence and courage. He collaborated with his co-pilot and calmly instructed his cabin crew to "brace for impact" to help manage the panic rising as a result of the terrible noises and jarring shudders of the aircraft, all in a matter of a few seconds.

Sully managed to land the plane successfully on water, with all crew and passengers safe, only 208 seconds after the bird strike. He was the last to evacuate the plane after having ensured everyone else was out and safe. This fortunate, unfortunate event changed aviation training protocols to include water landings.

For our purpose, we will look at Sully's demonstration of Responsibility and Proactivity, as they went hand in hand:

- First, he showed R1 (awareness of emotional states and their impact) and R2 (mastery in selecting emotions for effectiveness) by managing his own surge of dread on realizing what was happening.
- Then, he demonstrated R3 (making a life-affirming choice every time) when he chose to remain focused on assessing the possibilities.

- We see P1 (recognizing one's role in creating possibilities) when he made the bold choice to land in the river after taking the necessary time to consider all of the options.
- As he decided on a plan (P2 taking action by conscious choice), he maintained brief and purposeful communication with his co-pilot and cabin crew.
- He was mindful, not just of the message he was delivering, but also how he said the words, because he knew that any terror in his voice would be a sure way to add to the chaos (P3 demonstrating inner resilience). He needed everyone onboard to remain calm and focused, so he said only what was necessary: "Brace for impact."

The threat was real—it was an actual life-or-death matter. His decision and the way he carried it out affected 155 people, not to mention the ripple effect it had on their families. The pilots' commitment to one course of action and steady focus on lining up all the smaller actions necessary to land safely led them to make history in what will always be remembered as a modern-day miracle.

When actions, whether big or small, are focused in one direction, they will bear fruit in due time. Sometimes it takes years. What sustains you during the wait is the alignment with your big picture and the strength of your inner resilience.

Living by design: Up close and real

In this section, I share examples of meaningful journeys I've witnessed up close: my mother, Daad; the father of my children, Toufic; and my child, Karam. Each is from a different generation and background, yet all are grounded in the spirit of living life by design and not default.

Daad, baby boomer

The first example is my mother, Daad.

After finishing secondary school, Daad joined the Teacher Training Institute in Damascus, earned her certification, and began her career as an elementary school teacher. She got married at the age of twenty-one and had her first child at twenty-two. I followed four years later.

Daad worked full-time, with little to no help with her daily responsibilities, since my father worked double shifts at the time. Yet Daad held herself to high standards in everything she did. She was on top of things at work. At home, there were always home-cooked meals, and our place was neat, clean, and lovingly cared for. Creating a warm and welcoming space mattered deeply to her. She also managed to carve out time for deep, meaningful conversations with us, her children.

She loved people and cultivated a vibrant social circle, often connecting with expats from around the world who were living in Syria at the time. She attended cultural events, where she met interesting people and regularly invited them into our home. We grew up surrounded by friends from different parts of Europe, the United States, and Africa.

Teaching wasn't a job for her; it was a calling. Driven to grow professionally, she returned to school, earned her high school diploma, and later completed a bachelor's degree in English Language and Literature. This advancement led to a promotion as a high school English teacher. Her students loved and respected her. She cared for them far beyond the scope of administering the curriculum. Her mission wasn't just to teach language; it was to help shape her students' characters, grounded in integrity and compassion.

By the time she retired, both of her children had moved abroad. Still, she continued her legacy by supporting the children in her community, nurturing their curiosity and love of learning.

Daad had the same twenty-four hours as everyone else, but somehow she managed to do more with her time than most. She nurtured a family, built a rich social world, pursued higher education, and served her calling with excellence, all while staying anchored to her vision and principles. At seventy-four, she is still brimming with vitality, energy, and enthusiasm for life, now more than ever.

Toufic, Generation X

Toufic is the father of my children, and we shared eighteen years of our lives together. It was fascinating to witness what I can only describe as his "proactivity on steroids." With sharp business acumen and long-term vision, he built a successful enterprise and laid a strong foundation for the future, not only for our immediate family, but also our extended family and thousands of others. His accomplishments have earned him international recognition.

At an early age, Toufic became the sole provider for his family: his mother and three siblings. After finishing high school, his best friend's stepfather generously offered to pay for his university tuition, a gesture Toufic received with deep gratitude. He didn't take this help for granted. He found a job at the university and maintained high grades, eventually earning a partial scholarship to ease the financial burden on his benefactor.

Toufic dreamed of building a family bonded by love and connection, while also securing financial freedom for future generations. Twenty-five years later, he not only fulfilled that dream, but he exceeded it. He went on to establish a charitable foundation that supports children's education and provides medical treatment for those in need.

The path wasn't always clear for Toufic, but two things remained constant: his unwavering vision of where he was headed, and his deep faith in himself. He faced challenges, setbacks, and wrong turns, but he always found his way back, guided by a strong commitment to recovery and growth. Every day was a step forward, fueled by laser-beam focus, a sense of urgency, and intentional actions aligned with his bigger picture.

Three anchors contributed to Toufic's stellar success:

1. **Purposeful urgency:** He moved with intention and speed, always ahead of the curve, addressing things before they became problems.
2. **Solid priorities:** He had a clear sense of what mattered most, and he honored those priorities consistently.
3. **Disciplined self-care:** Taking care of himself was part of his daily routine; not something reserved only for vacations or free time.

Toufic continues to shape new dreams and move toward them with intention. Creating possibilities and taking action in alignment with his vision has become his natural way of living.

Karam, Generation Z

Karam, my third child, was seventeen years old when I wrote this book. He had a speech delay until he was two and a half years old, and he needed speech and language therapy during the first few years of school. He switched into proactivity at a very young age.

In primary school, his teachers often commented on his difficulty staying focused. One teacher once said to me, "He's daydreaming most of the time in class."

I asked Karam about it, and he said, "School is boring, Mom. My favorite time there is break time."

Karam began exploring activities outside of school that might interest him. He tried basketball, karate, tennis, and jujitsu until he eventually found his passion in boxing, and later, in theater and performing arts.

Before his seventeenth birthday, he had already competed in four club-level boxing matches, winning three. He also played the lead role in his school's production of the Shrek musical, delivering a performance that, as his teachers remarked, suggested a star in the making. He trained diligently for nine months, preparing his voice and presence to shine in the spotlight, and shine he did. Although he was late to start speaking, Karam eventually found his voice in ways that far exceeded expectations.

In secondary school, a teacher approached me with a very different concern from those voiced in his earlier years. "I'm a bit worried about Karam," he said. "He told me that he wakes up at 5:30 a.m. to go for a run before school. He's very strict about his diet and said he works out six days a week." I thanked the teacher for his concern and asked, "What exactly worries you about that?" He responded, "Don't get me wrong, I spoke to Karam. I know this is 100% his choice and that you didn't impose it. It's just… this lifestyle sounds too much for someone his age. I can't imagine living like that."

In that moment, I remembered a line from *The Pursuit of Happyness* movie where Chris Gardner, played by Will Smith, tells his son, "People can't do something themselves, they want to tell you 'you can't do it.'"[15] I thanked the teacher again for reaching out and, respectfully, suggested he focus on the other 1,999 students in the school and let Karam be. This kid had himself sorted out. He knew exactly what he was doing and why.

Today, I see Karam finding joy in balancing his study schedule, workout routine, theater practice, and vocal, guitar, and dance training, while also spending quality time with family and friends. He eats well, sleeps well, and manages it all with steady self-discipline. His focus in class has increased significantly. He thinks long-term, and he builds himself from the inside out. He asks thoughtful questions, seeks to grow, and develops life skills intentionally and consistently. Beyond all that, he carries a cheerful presence that lights up the room.

Each of the three examples—Daad, Toufic, and Karam—refuses to live by default. They create possibilities for themselves that aren't immediately available, and they take actions aligned with a big picture they have defined for themselves. Each navigates challenges with eyes focused on what lies ahead.

Proactivity can take many forms that are personal and unique to each individual, and it isn't limited to adulthood. How you express it is entirely your business. From a catalytic point of view, the only guideline is this: live life by your own design.

Being proactive in one area of life doesn't necessarily mean you are in all areas. So, the question remains: how can you expand your proactivity? It's a lifelong, dynamic process.

The Way of the Catalyst is to set yourself free of the limitations of your current reality by creating new possibilities inspired by your Big Picture Personal Canvas and consciously choosing to take a deliberate action to realize a determined outcome. It is crucial to define what is important for you first, setting your priorities and creating a set of guidelines for what you will do or not do, and how. This level of clarity enhances your inner resilience to withstand obstacles along the way.

Catalysts are focused people who make their own lives into works of art, touch the lives of others, and steer every experience with their commitment to excellence.

Proactivity: Proficiency level 5

What it usually sounds like:

- I think in every situation. I have a choice and can shape the outcome to the extent that is within my control.
- There are resources not immediately evident, which is why I ensure that I find out the possibilities ahead of time before I attempt anything.
- I have a sense of urgency to move forward, but it stems more from direction than from restlessness.
- I view conflict as an opportunity to improve.
- It is necessary to say "no" if needed for the bigger picture of what is to be achieved. However, one does not have to be disagreeable to disagree.
- I am able to look at life objectively.
- Teamwork means that everyone needs to pull their weight.

- I am aware of the present circumstances, but I don't let them negatively influence how I view the future or plan my actions.
- I am respectful and mindful of policies, and I don't let them become an obstacle.
- When I can't perform something, I look for someone with the right experience and expertise who is effective at achieving goals, realizing the vision, and solving problems, and I collaborate with them to make progress.

P1: Recognizing one's own role in creating possibilities

The consistent ability to draw guidance for present thoughts, beliefs, and actions from a reality that is shaped by the Big Picture Personal Canvas while being mindful of the present.

What it usually sounds like:

- In any situation, I like first to check the various possibilities before acting accordingly.
- I am able to sense the feelings and perspectives of others, take an active interest in their concerns, and see how I can be of service. This helps us succeed together.

- I am always guided by a sense of purpose and take actions that align with the bigger picture. If my big picture includes other people and we're collaborating, our big pictures need to integrate together, incorporating the larger good.
- I am able to step outside my comfort zone as often as I need to, and I do so for a larger benefit.
- I am able to share a vision of the future, a possible outcome, and an alternate version of an approach, so that I can help others look beyond the mundane, even in their own lives.
- I think it is important to be excited about what life has to offer. This helps to create passion and inspiration to look beyond present constraints or perspectives, and I've seen how actions change when this happens.
- I am patient and compassionate toward people who want to be a better version of themselves, and I do what I can within reasonable limits to support them without interfering with their lives.

P2: Taking action by conscious choice

The consistent ability to ensure that every action one takes comes from a mindful assessment of choices that are aligned with the Big Picture Personal Canvas one desires.

What it usually sounds like:

- When working with others, I am able to show respect, helpfulness, and cooperation, drawing people into active and enthusiastic participation.
- I urge people (including myself) to be empowered to make choices and not to be driven by the tide or go with the flow because everyone seems to be doing it.
- I know that I have the ability to influence the direction of my life through my own choices and actions.
- I prefer to use words that are uplifting, encouraging, and positive, focusing on hope and possibilities. I don't need to use negative language to acknowledge that sometimes things go a different way.
- I am aware of my reality, but not limited by it.
- I am able to extend my thinking and abilities beyond the present when it comes to acquiring knowledge and experiences that shape my future.
- When it involves others, I can focus less on my needs, without compromise, and work for the greater good of all.
- I usually enjoy taking the initiative, actively shaping my reality instead of just reacting to it. My thoughts, words, and actions are conscious choices I make every day.

P3: Demonstrating inner resilience

The consistent ability to follow through with one's actions while remaining fully mindful of and withstanding the consequences or outcomes that follow those actions. In doing so, one demonstrates an inner resilience.

What it usually sounds like:

- I know that in the larger picture of life, I have more control over myself than others.
- I am concerned with being a stronger person from within. I face my fears actively and responsibly.
- Rather than focusing on personality, which is on the outside, I focus on building character, which is on the inside.
- I base my life on how "things can be" and live my life using that frame of reference. This gives me the strength to navigate any kind of situation I face.
- I don't hesitate to seek help and leverage the experience and wisdom of those around me (irrespective of age, background, creed, etc.) in effective ways to achieve goals and realize a vision.

Key points

- Proactivity: Living life by design:
  - P1: Recognizing one's own role in creating possibilities.
  - P2: Taking action by conscious choice.
  - P3: Demonstrating inner resilience.
- Changing an outcome requires clarity on the desired state, conscious and consistent action, inner resilience, and grit to stay the course.
- Integrated Time Awareness unlocks your ability to live by design.
- Creating a mental space means repurposing your energy, reorganizing your priorities, reallocating your time, and filtering your relationships, thoughts, and activities, so that you keep only what matters.
- Knowing what you're doing and why matters. When you lose sight of the big picture, pause, reset, and then resume.
- The best time to learn life skills is before you need them, when there's calm and relative stability.
- Focused actions eventually bear fruit, though sometimes it can take years. What keeps you

going while you wait is the alignment with your big picture and the strength of your inner resilience.

- When you refuse to live by default, you create possibilities that aren't immediately available, take actions that are aligned with your big picture, and navigate challenges with your eyes focused on what lies ahead.
- Being proactive in one area of life doesn't necessarily mean you are in all areas. Seeking to expand your proactivity is a lifelong, dynamic process.
- It is crucial to begin by defining what is important for you, setting your priorities, and creating a set of guidelines as to what you will do or not do, and how.

5

Interdependence: Sharing Power With All Involved

Life on our planet continues because all living things are interconnected in an interdependent relationship. Different organisms engage with each other, all fulfilling their roles to create life as we know it.

Nature has an innate ability to recover itself to a state of interdependence, an ecological balance where all beings co-exist in synergy. Coral reefs regenerate after bleaching events, forests regrow after wildfires, and fish populations rebound when human pressure is reduced.

Our bodies are no different. They operate at a high level of interdependence, with each organ doing its part to sustain life within us. When some cells go awry, our entire system is affected, triggering signals for recovery and repair. Most of the time, this healing happens naturally, unless the disturbance is too great for the body to manage alone and it requires external support to restore balance.

Interdependence for the Catalyst

Catalysts understand that to be sustainably effective in leadership, relationships, and life in general, they must stand firmly in their own power while allowing space for others to do the same. Rather than competing with or diminishing themselves or others, Catalysts recognize that power multiplies when it is shared. They operate from the belief that through co-creating with others, they can achieve far more than they ever could alone.

In contrast, some leadership approaches focus heavily on conformity and obedience, which suppresses creativity, psychological safety, and responsiveness to change in groups. Catalysts take a different path, amplifying the collective potential by encouraging autonomy and independent thinking. That is the essence of power shared. Interdependence does not diminish individuality; it celebrates differences and brings them into purposeful collaboration.

Catalysts are acutely aware of their unique skills, vulnerabilities, responsibilities, and the impact they have. Moreover, they actively create the conditions for others to step into their power by fostering an environment of safety, trust, and openness. This way of being naturally paves the way for Influence (the fourth attitude of the Catalyst—coming in the next chapter). Catalysts recognize that when each person fully owns their role, the collective becomes greater than the sum of its parts. Together, they form a unified and harmonious whole, alive and dynamic by nature.

Three traits of Interdependence

Interdependence is the third attitude of the Catalyst and is expressed through three interwoven traits:

- I1: Confidence in oneself
- I2: Comfort with vulnerability
- I3: Accepting of differences

The Catalyst's self-confidence emanates from a dynamic inner source that is not attached to status, titles, achievements, or possessions. It reveals itself in their ability to transition fluidly between dependence (relying on others), independence (relying on themselves), and interdependence (co-creating with others in a balanced interaction in which power is respected, granted, and shared). This agility strengthens the system's ability to function effectively, even under pressure and in times of crisis.

Vulnerability can be real or perceived. In either case, it has an impact on behaviors and actions. The Catalyst uses vulnerability as a means to gain collaborative strength. Instead of dominating conversations, Catalysts invite others' perspectives, knowing that diverse viewpoints enrich the outcome. In meetings, they intentionally create space for quieter voices to contribute, ensuring everyone's input is valued. In decision-making, they share ownership of the process, trusting that collaboration breeds stronger, more resilient solutions.

In high-intensity situations, Catalysts respond to the needs of the moment, whether by taking a directive approach tempered with respect and compassion or an accommodating approach bolstered by integrity and power. Their self-awareness and commitment to the big picture allow them to navigate situations and relationships in rich, meaningful ways.

Catalysts appreciate that each person brings a unique set of strengths and vulnerabilities. They thrive on the understanding that when every contribution is respected and integrated, the whole system becomes richer, more dynamic, and more resilient. They recognize their role within the larger whole and take full responsibility for preparing themselves mentally, emotionally, and practically to fulfill their part, without needing reminders or external pressure. In both personal and professional life, this self-driven readiness builds trust, strengthens relationships, and sets a standard of excellence that encourages others to give their best contribution.

Interdependence in art

Imagine a magnificent painting that presents a vivid interplay of individual colors and shapes, each contributing to the larger composition. Every color holds its own identity, each clear and distinct. Every shape has its own borders and lines. Yet, no color or shape on its own is capable of giving the same impression as the composition as a whole. The combination of contrasting colors and expressive shapes tells a story that brings the painting to life as a coherent whole. What is experienced as beauty is not the dominance of any one but the synergy between them, each enhancing and elevating the other.

Imagine an orchestra of a hundred musicians, each playing their part to bring a symphony to life. Every instrument carries its own distinct sound. Each musician masters their individual role, yet their contribution alone would be incomplete without the others. Each sound weaves into the next, creating a layered, dynamic tapestry of music. The beauty of the performance emerges from this intricate interdependence, where every musician listens, adjusts, and responds to the whole. The brilliance of the symphony is born not from one sound, but from the interaction between them all.

Imagine a world-class dance performance, with fifty dancers on stage, each moving with precision and grace. Every dancer is fully attuned to their own body, to the rhythm of the music, and to the subtle cues of those around them. No one performer dominates the stage; instead, each movement blends into a larger choreography, creating a living, breathing work of art.

Interdependence is what transforms single performances into a unified whole in which timing, space, and energy flow seamlessly between them. Without this deep mutual attunement, the performance would fall apart, but when interdependence is honored, something breathtaking comes to life.

In each of these examples—the painting, the orchestra, and the dance performance—interdependence is not about losing individuality. It's quite the opposite. Every color must hold its richness, every musician must master their instrument, and every dancer must embody their craft with strength and precision. Independence is the first step toward interdependence. Only when each part is sufficiently developed on its own can it fully engage with the larger fabric of the interdependent group.

True interdependence is an interplay between wholeness and connection, where individuals, strong and confident in themselves, come together to create something far greater than they could achieve alone.

Interdependence in interactions

Whether you're stepping forward to lead (see the case study of Mr. F) or stepping back to allow space for others (see my story afterward), true power is staying attuned to the moment and being ready to shift gears as needed, without slipping into exaggerated responsibility or extreme detachment.

CASE STUDY: Choosing to be heard—the power of speaking up

Mr. F was recently promoted to lead a major cross-functional project at his company. It was the kind of role he had dreamed about. But when he sat at the roundtable with the directors and senior managers, he felt the familiar pull: "Should I play it safe and agree? Should I speak up? Should I wait to see which way the wind is blowing?"

At the first few meetings, he found himself nodding along with the majority, even though his instincts whispered otherwise. He noticed tension building inside him, a growing sense of disconnection from himself.

One afternoon, after a particularly draining meeting at which a critical decision was made without addressing a major risk he had seen, Mr. F had a session with his coach. This situation became the focus of their conversation.

Mr. F realized that by withholding his voice, he was abandoning not just the project's potential, but also his integrity. He chose to make peace with the feeling of vulnerability that came with challenging the group direction, a risk he needed to take to stay true to his role in the project.

He was aware that the group could dismiss his input. But this wasn't about imposing his views; it was about bringing his perspective to the table clearly and respectfully, and letting it stand on its own.

At the next meeting, when the conversation drifted toward another decision that seemed rushed, Mr. F calmly spoke up, "I hear the urgency. And I'd like to share a risk that I think deserves our attention before we move forward." The room went silent for a moment, and then they started asking questions and exploring new angles.

Some didn't agree with his point, and that was fine. What mattered was that he stood in his power without needing to dominate or withdraw. He spoke up in service of both his personal big picture and driving the project toward sustainable success, remaining true to himself even in difficult or uncertain situations.

Over time, his consistency built trust. Colleagues started inviting his perspective earlier. Even when they disagreed with him, they respected his clarity. Mr. F had become a Catalyst in his group, bringing confidence, vulnerability, and acceptance all at once.

There were moments, especially when my four children were younger, when sitting around the dinner table felt less like family time and more like a debate tournament. Four voices were chiming in, each with its own emotional tone, tempo, and personality. One would interrupt another, someone else would shut down completely, and the volume often rose with the intensity of the day's feelings.

I couldn't tolerate this auditory mess. I would rush to intervene, deliver a verdict, and force harmony back around the table. This hardly ever worked, at least not without more drama erupting. My children would end up not only angry with each other, but also with me. Something wasn't working, but I didn't know exactly what. Was it a clash between their different temperaments and communication styles? Was it how I intervened?

Determined to find a better way, I joined a course on effective parenting and devoured every book I could find. I knew what I wanted—harmony and peace in our home—and I needed a method for the madness.

I learned that the more I tried to solve the debate for them, the more I fed the tension. Their arguments were, in fact, an essential part of their development; that's how they were learning about themselves, what mattered to them, and how to engage with the outer world as they grew older. There was a brilliant opportunity hidden inside the chaos, one I had been unknowingly suppressing by trying to fix things too soon, before they were developmentally ready to extract the learning embedded in the experience.

Loving those kids more than life itself, I made a hard but conscious choice to step back and allow them the space to grow through resolving their challenges, with me in the background if they needed me. It wasn't easy, especially at the beginning. They were used to me stepping in. When I didn't, they would complain, trying to pull me back into the familiar role of referee. I would gently say, "I know you're old enough to sort this out. You try first. You've got this. I'm here if you need me."

It took time, a great deal of patience, and even more self-control to let them work it out. But they did. They still have their moments, of course, but the bond they've built is truly admirable. Stepping back and trusting their ability to think for themselves and come up with creative solutions that worked for them allowed them to grow their confidence in navigating the outer world, find ease in uncomfortable situations, and discover their unique style of handling differences and disagreements.

All it took was for me to step back from my own need to "rescue" and instead sit with the discomfort of their conflicts, without rushing in for a quick fix. I learned to appreciate my vulnerability in those moments, and to trust the real, often messy, unfolding of their psychological growth.

Both of the stories above—one around the meeting table, the other around the dinner table—reveal different expressions of the same truth. Standing in your own power is not about control or dominance; it's about showing up with confidence and vulnerability, accepting differing viewpoints, and being unattached to the outcome.

Whether you're stepping forward to lead or stepping back to allow space for others, true power is staying attuned to what is needed in the moment and being ready to shift gears. This range—the ability to stand firm in your own power, recognize the power of others, and move with confidence, vulnerability, and acceptance—is at the heart of Interdependence.

Interdependence in delegation

The illusion of having to do it all alone often leads to depletion and burnout. Delegation is more than task distribution; it's an act of interdependence and building capacity through others. Let's look at the case of Ms. G by way of example.

CASE STUDY: Atlas syndrome—when independence becomes dysfunctional

Ms. G is a dear friend of mine. She is a single mother with a demanding full-time job, and her work often spills into the evenings. She avoids taking vacations because, in her words, "I end up paying the price for taking a break. I come back to a mountain of backlog."

She insists on making home-cooked meals for her daughter, is hands-on at work, and is committed to supporting her retired parents. Somehow, she still makes time to nurture friendships. I've never seen her drop the ball, not at work, home, or in her relationships. But I've seen the toll it's taking on her.

During an online meeting, a co-worker from another department tried to shift part of his workload to her. She snapped. It wasn't just frustration; it was a full-on meltdown. Later, the managing director, who had personally hired her years before and deeply valued her work ethic, called her privately. "I know you're under pressure," he said. "The company has grown, and the workload isn't what it was when you joined us thirteen years ago. You're still handling all our supplier-client transactions and billing alone. How about you build a small team to support you? Start with two people and see how it goes."

She declined, saying, "Thank you, but training new people takes time, and right now it will only add to the pressure. I honestly can't take that on."

I wasn't surprised. Ms. G is so meticulous that she finds it hard to trust others to meet her standards. Rather than delegate, she chose once again to shoulder the load alone. But as time passed, more cracks began to show. She became visibly exhausted, less focused, and increasingly tense, both at work and at home. Conversations with her began to feel like navigating a minefield.

Eventually, concerned friends and family gently intervened. They pointed out the obvious: this wasn't sustainable. She finally agreed to hire two people, trained them, and began to let go. To her surprise, not only did her team rise to the occasion, but they adopted her eye for detail and even introduced improvements to the workflow.

Ms. G had always prided herself on being independent, and she was, but her independence had crossed a line. It was no longer serving her or those around her. It wasn't until she allowed herself to lean on others and embrace interdependence that her independence started to work for her again.

She had to acknowledge her limits and vulnerability, not from a place of neediness or helplessness (which would have been dysfunctional dependence), but from a place of creating greater harmony and balance, both at work and home.

She still believes her way is the best—and it probably is. However, now she appreciates that other valid approaches exist too. By creating space for others to contribute, she has discovered the power of delegation and teamwork.

I've seen versions of Ms. G's story many times in different contexts: new parents unwilling to accept help because "no one does it like I do," leaders who can't delegate without anxiety, caregivers who refuse support until they're utterly depleted, and individuals with chronic illnesses who resist exploring new options that might ease their path.

Interdependence is not about giving up control; it's about recognizing when our fierce independence has become a cage and choosing, instead, to open the door.

Five-step process to develop Interdependence as a catalytic attitude

Next, let us consider the five-step process to help you develop the catalytic attitude of Interdependence in practical terms.

Step one: Master your roles

Whether you're a leader, employee, partner, friend, student, or contributor in any capacity, focus on developing the ability to perform your roles effectively, fully, and completely. The value you gain goes far beyond external achievements. Your capacity to grow builds your self-confidence. The real reward lies in your ability to learn and evolve.

Step two: Leverage others' strengths

You don't have to do it all alone or have all the answers. Having clarity about your own limits helps you see others' complementary strengths. Notice where others naturally shine, ask for their input, delegate with trust, and remain open to approaches that differ from yours. When people feel seen and valued for what they bring, they step up, and the whole system gets stronger.

Step three: Learn to be comfortable in uncomfortable situations

Discomfort is often a sign of growth, change, or truth unfolding. You might feel the urge to relieve the tension too soon, unintentionally depriving yourself of the gift it carries. Tolerate discomfort long enough for you to learn something about yourself. Your limits and vulnerabilities open the space for collaboration, as we saw in Ms. G's story.

Step four: Find at least one thing to appreciate

While some people are harder to appreciate than others, there's almost always at least one thing you can recognize and value about them. Choosing to notice that one thing can shift the energy of an interaction, sometimes without you even saying a word. It helps soften your stance just enough to create space for a more constructive exchange.

Step five: Navigate tension without collapsing or dominating

Name the tension. Call it out calmly, without blame or drama. Say what you notice: "It feels like something is off here, are you OK?" or, "I sense some resistance, can we talk about it?" Naming what's happening gives everyone permission to drop the performance and be real.

Stay curious and ask open-ended questions. Be willing to explore what's beneath the surface, whether that is assumptions, fears, or unmet needs. Curiosity opens the door to empathy and often reveals solutions that everyone can get behind.

Keep it real. Don't sugarcoat or shrink to make others comfortable, but don't bulldoze either. Speak your truth with clarity and care, and hold compassion for others if they can't mirror your openness. It is possible that they can't see what you see.

Allow time. Not everything can be resolved in one conversation. Tension takes time to unwind. Sometimes space is needed before a breakthrough can happen. Don't confuse silence with failure. Give the process breathing room.

The fruits of Interdependence are more than can be written in these pages. The variety is as expansive as life itself. Simply put, Interdependence allows for life and growth to flow freely in any system that secures it. It is at the center of all Five Attitudes of the Catalyst, because you step out of your own personal space of Responsibility and Proactivity, into the social space of Interdependence, followed by Influence and Excellence.

The Five Attitudes are intertwined to form a way of living, individually and collectively, in the social space. Inner balance precedes outer balance and forms the foundation for gaining collaborative strength.

Interdependence: Proficiency level 5

What it usually sounds like:

- I am assertive all the time, and it's never only about me.
- I know when someone else can do a better job than I, and I make every attempt to get them involved.
- I know when I am great at something, and I am usually given the opportunity to do it.
- I make sure everyone has the opportunity to do what they can do best.
- I am able to stand up for what I believe in gently without being nasty.
- I am able to encourage others to speak up or step back when necessary.
- It's great to be surrounded by people who are smarter or more knowledgeable, talented, or skilled than I am.
- I discuss outcomes or results, then match people to the abilities needed and discuss how we can work effectively.
- I can remain calm and objective, even during difficult times, to make sure that authority and ability are used to enable rather than control or suppress.

I1: Confidence in oneself

The consistent ability to demonstrate mindful dependence, independence, and interdependence, where self-confidence is from a dynamic source within that provides power, strength, guidance, and comfort.

What it usually sounds like:

- My confidence is not sourced from my past achievements and material elements. It is based on my quest to master myself.
- I am open to and accommodating of different values, opinions, and beliefs. They don't affect the way I perceive myself or my life.
- I am always assertive, being mindful of those around me. I show openness to and acceptance of others sharing their ideas. I speak up when necessary and encourage others to do the same.
- I welcome constructive conflict and navigate it with calm, clarity, and the communication skills needed to find a resolution.
- I know my limitations and quickly leverage the capabilities of people around me.
- I delegate authority along with responsibility.
- I initiate change in myself first when needed.

- Even when I'm unsure of the outcome, I'm clear on how I'll navigate it, staying true to myself, with integrity and balance.

12: Comfort with vulnerability

The consistent ability to recognize when one is vulnerable, acknowledge its impact on oneself and how it shapes behavior, and use it as a means to harness collaborative strengths.

What it usually sounds like:

- When I don't know the answer, I back it up with what I do know or have studied, or what I am going to do about it.
- Vulnerability can be converted into a source of strength and an opportunity for collaboration and discovery. I am encouraged by it, and I help others see it that way too.
- I am happy not to know all the answers and to be surrounded by knowledgeable, talented, and skilled people.
- When I know someone is vulnerable or has expressed vulnerability (directly or subtly), I create a space for them to be themselves.
- I welcome difficult conversations and take the interpersonal initiative in asking for help,

support, or guidance when needed, because that's the way forward.

- When I make mistakes, I am quick to recognize them (on my own or from feedback), acknowledge them gracefully and appropriately (to all affected), and make consistent efforts to work on them.
- I know that it is in the long run that character evolves. Thus, I remain consistent in word, action, and behavior during difficult or testing times. This builds trust.

13: Accepting of differences

The consistent ability to adapt one's response, while being mindful of how others perceive their reality, in order to build collaborative strength.

What it usually sounds like:

- Within reasonable limits, I let people be, and I think it is necessary for people to have their own opinions or ideas, even if they are different.
- I am committed to seeking to understand first, in order to ensure I interpret correctly and with little or no bias or prejudice.
- I am able to objectively visualize the outcome of a discussion, and I don't feel the need to pursue a negotiation when people have opposing ideas.

- I prefer to use dialogue to create a trusting environment and to use differences for self-analysis and improvement.
- I recognize that different people have different ways and means of contributing.
- When there is a difference, I approach it with curiosity and can examine situations from different perspectives and contexts rather than using a "one size fits all" approach.
- Especially at times of conflict, I know that preserving self-respect, diversity of opinion, and inclusion are important in the long run.
- I am able to remember that there is a reason why people behave the way they do and, within reasonable limits, I am supportive.
- I am not limited by past experiences, prejudices, rules, or beliefs, and I can examine what is beneficial now and for the future.

Key points

- Interdependence: Sharing power with all involved:
  - I1: Confidence in oneself.
  - I2: Comfort with vulnerability.
  - I3: Accepting of differences.

- At Interdependence, you step out of your inner world into the social space.
- Interdependence does not diminish individuality; it celebrates differences and brings them into purposeful collaboration.
- When each person fully owns their role, the collective becomes greater than the sum of its parts.
- The self-confidence of a Catalyst emanates from a dynamic inner source, unattached to status, titles, achievements, or possessions.
- Vulnerability can be real or perceived. In both cases, it has an impact on behaviors and actions.
- Independence is the first step toward Interdependence.
- Standing in your own power is not about exerting control or dominance. It's about showing up with confidence and vulnerability while staying unattached to the outcomes.
- Interdependence is not about giving up control either. It's about recognizing when our fierce independence has become a cage and choosing to open the door.
- Interdependence allows for life and growth to flow freely in any system that secures it.

6

Influence: Causing An Effect Without Force

To move a glass of water from one side of the table to the other, you simply need to exert force and push it to where you want it to be. Unlike living beings, the glass has no will of its own to resist.

In leadership, when used mindfully and purposefully, force is a great approach to managing emergencies, disrupting toxic patterns, and enforcing order and structure in chaotic situations. However, how you use any tool matters. The knife in the hand of an experienced surgeon gives life, while in a murderer's hand, it takes away life. In the same way, there's a difference between force used as a supportive and directive tool and force that is a default power-over tactic.

While force produces obedience and drives quicker outcomes, it suppresses others' growth and commitment. It is a fear-based approach that moves people in a direction that has been determined for them. Some authority figures, such as leaders, managers, and parents, rely solely on force in the pursuit of immediate compliance, sacrificing trust and long-term, constructive impact. This not only diminishes the growth, creativity, and well-being of those they lead but also erodes their own credibility, influence, and effectiveness.

In relationships, force takes the shape of control through angry outbursts, emotional blackmail, manipulation, and psychological games, the outcome of which is painful and deadening for all involved. These patterns take place when individuals cannot recognize options to have their needs met in a healthy and constructive manner. This was examined in depth by Eric Berne in his book, *Games People Play*.[16]

Influence, on the other hand, engages people's hearts and minds and transforms their lives through inspiration and empowerment. Through the catalyst lens, it's not just about what you say or do; it's about who you are on the inside and what you emanate to the outside. The first three attitudes make your catalytic impact—Influence—possible:

1. Taking charge of inner thoughts, emotions, and stories (Responsibility)

2. Living life by design (Proactivity)
3. Sharing power with all involved (Interdependence)

Unlike force that pressures from the outside, influence sparks change from within, driving momentum to shape a future that's beyond current circumstances or limitations.

Three traits of Influence

Influence is the fourth attitude of the catalyst and is expressed through the following three interwoven traits:

- F1: Navigating disarray in oneself and others
- F2: Creating effective safe spaces
- F3: Tailoring communication to the listener

Influence expands the Catalyst's attitude of Responsibility to include taking charge of their impact in the social space. Through an intentional choice of words, actions, and behaviors, the Catalyst creates a safe space to cultivate the conditions for evolution, alignment, and meaningful transformation in themselves and others. Making this kind of impact requires empathy, presence, and clarity. Catalysts do not just move people to action; they ignite momentum, add meaning, and inspire a shift in perspective.

CASE STUDY: When globalization gets personal

Dr. H is a university professor in political science. She believes that if you're not enjoying what you're studying, then you're not learning. For her, the ultimate purpose of learning is to transform individuals and enable them to co-create a better world. Since childhood, she has been fascinated by different cultures. She has travelled around the world and immersed herself in the cultural traditions of countries she has visited, from East to West. Besides English, her mother tongue, she has learned multiple languages, such as Portuguese, Arabic, Hebrew, and Italian. She appreciates authentic food, music, and even TV shows of different cultures.

She was teaching a course in globalization for international politics students. On the first day of class, she noticed that her students perceived the subject as abstract and distant. For them, "globalization" seemed to equate with eating burgers, wearing jeans, and posting on social media. They couldn't connect with the political or economic aspects of it. There was hardly any engagement, and many looked like they had something more interesting on their mobile phones. The class was not going well.

Dr. H decided to shift her approach and make it personal. She put up a photo on the screen from one of her trips to a village in Africa. It looked very different from the neat, modern classroom where the class was taking place. In the background of the photo, a bus was parked on the side of a dirt road. Travel bags and wrapped cloth bundles were scattered on the ground next to the bus, and people in traditional clothes were waiting around. In front of the bus, two local men smiled at the camera.

Dr. H said, “This is a photo from my trip to Cameroon to do research on waste management. The man on the right is Mr. J, my colleague. He’s a professor. The one on the left is a researcher. In this photo, we were waiting to take the bus to travel from Buea to Bamenda, an eight-hour ride. The night before, I asked Mr. J what time the bus would leave, and he said, ‘In the morning.’

“I said, ‘OK, but when?’

“He replied, ‘When the bus is full.’

“That baffled me. I said, ‘Wouldn’t it be more efficient if buses had a set time?’

“He said, ‘Dear, this is Africa.’

“Later that day, Mr. J asked me whether globalization was good or bad for Africa. What would you tell Mr. J? There’s no right or wrong answer here. What are your thoughts?”

The students started a debate. Some said, “It’s bad because the people will lose their culture,” while others countered, “But they need infrastructure, modernization, and investment.”

The photo and the story inspired those young adults to start thinking beyond themselves. They were not just consuming content; they were engaging, feeling, questioning, and exploring the gray area between right and wrong.

> In under two minutes, Dr. H opened a window to the world, stimulating her students' minds. She demonstrated a powerful example of Influence that goes beyond passing on information. Many of the students told her at the end of the session that it had been very interesting. She was satisfied and grateful to see a light in their eyes and the spark of curiosity she had been hoping to ignite.

Let's examine the story through the lens of the Catalyst.

Dr. H recognized the students' lack of connection with the course subject, shifted the traditional learning approach, and captured their attention in a meaningful way (F1: navigating disarray in oneself and others).

Notice that she was the authority figure in the room. She could have used force. She could have told the students to put their phones away. Instead, she created an inviting space for exploration and discovery by sharing a relevant personal experience that brought an abstract subject to life (F2: creating effective safe spaces).

She bridged two worlds, connecting her students to people they had never met, while stimulating their thinking and welcoming their ideas without judgment. They left the class that day not just more informed but more aware and more human than when they had entered (F3: tailoring communication to the listener).

Influence from OKness

OKness is a core concept in Transactional Analysis (TA). TA, founded by Eric Berne in the 1950s, is a theory of personality and systemic psychotherapy for personal growth and personal change, aiming to promote awareness, autonomy, and healthy communication in therapy, coaching, education, leadership, and everyday life. Thomas Harris popularized the concept of OKness in his bestselling book, *I'm OK, You're OK.*[17] OKness describes how people see themselves and others in interactions. It means acknowledging worthiness, resourcefulness, and wholeness in oneself and in others.

When Influence comes from an "I'm OK, You're OK" position, it shifts from pressure to power, opening the possibility for change and movement through insight, inspiration, and resonance. It becomes a pure expression of the self that extends to growing and expanding others into better versions of themselves.

You might be thinking, "What about people who have done bad things? How can I see them as worthy, resourceful, and whole?" Seeing others as OK does not mean tolerating abuse, underperformance, or harmful behavior. It also doesn't mean pretending everything is fine, over-adapting, discounting your pain, or forgiving when you're not ready. "I'm OK, You're OK" does not let people off the hook. It allows you to say "no" with dignity, set boundaries, ask for what you need, make conscious choices, and maintain a state of integrity, relational balance, and inner harmony. It liberates you from resentment, overwhelm, guilt, shame, and insecurity.

It becomes possible when you separate the person from the behavior, recognizing that others, just like you, are shaped by their experience and level of awareness. One of the most powerful applications of "I'm OK, You're OK" is to help release you from the excuses you might make for yourself or others when tolerating what's imposed on you without your consent, such as the unsolicited dumping of emotional baggage into your space. Instead, you can see yourself as the capable person you are and allow others to take responsibility for their choices while maintaining inner safety and communicating with clarity and assertiveness.

It is important to make the distinction here between tolerance as a dysfunctional choice that enables harmful behavior and suppresses change, and benign tolerance as a functional option that aligns with the big picture and permits sustainability, nurturing, connection, growth, and progress, without compromising principles or well-being.

CASE STUDY: OKness in action

Mr. K was the owner of a small social media marketing agency. When the business started growing, he hired a social media director to lead the team so that he could focus on business development. He found what seemed to be the perfect candidate who had extensive experience, a strategic mindset, and a sharp eye for detail. The new director stepped in confidently and quickly created the space that Mr. K needed to acquire new clients and expand the agency's offerings.

A few months in, Mr. K started to notice that the director's forceful leadership style, masked as "tough love," was gradually eroding the team's energy and morale. Engagement dropped, creativity stalled, and people seemed to be playing it safe. These were clear signs that psychological safety was at risk.

Concerned, Mr. K invited the director for a meeting. "Thank you for the effort you've been putting into your role," he said. "I recognize that leading a growing team isn't easy. Recently, I've noticed some concerning signs: the team seems less engaged, and there's been a noticeable dip in idea sharing and openness. That tells me something in the environment might not feel safe enough for people to fully show up. I'd like us to explore that honestly together. From your perspective, what's been going on? And how do you see your role in shifting things toward a healthier team culture?"

The director explained that he was holding the team to high standards and focusing on building a culture of accountability. The conversation led to a clear agreement on the next steps—offering constructive feedback in private rather than during team meetings and adopting a tone that fosters clarity, connection, and trust, while steering clear of any shaming.

The director followed through for a few weeks, then slipped back into old patterns. Mr. K invited him for a second conversation, pointing out his inconsistency and the ongoing impact on the team dynamics.

The director grew defensive and didn't offer any solution. Mr. K held him accountable for the need to lead the team in a way that was effective and aligned with the company's values. He asked him to reflect on their conversation, define clear leadership standards for himself, and return with a response that demonstrated his alignment with the company's culture.

Three weeks passed with no visible change. In fact, the director's behavior escalated. Mr. K made the decision to let him go. Like many others, the director was hired for his expertise and fired for his attitude.

This experience prompted Mr. K to refine his hiring process by placing greater emphasis on cultural fit and background checks alongside skills and experience. Today, he has built a culture that values both results and relationships. While the incident initially slowed progress, it ultimately cleared the path for faster and healthier growth.

Mr. K demonstrated an 'I'm OK, You're OK' stance throughout—initiating a difficult conversation, setting clear expectations, making a respectful request, and even navigating a contract termination. When the director became defensive, Mr. K maintained steady composure and allowed time for resolution. He refused to accept results that left behind a trail of burnout and disengagement. By honoring both task and people, he stayed true to his company's core values.

Common challenges for Influence

Catalysts do not see influence as something they do; it's who they are. The way they live their lives plants seeds of transformation within others in their orbit. The challenges for catalytic Influence arise from within the self, not from the outside world. Here's what gets in the way of living the three traits of Influence.

F1: Navigating disarray in oneself and others

Disarray comes with difficult feelings, such as overwhelm, shame, grief, confusion, embarrassment, inadequacy, hostility, discouragement, and skepticism. A lack of emotional intelligence and self-regulation makes it hard to sit with those emotions, whether they are yours or others'. Some people suppress their own emotions and those of others because they don't know what to do in such moments. They lack the tools. Some use the idea of "positivity" as an excuse to ignore problems in their lives and their relationships. In short, fear of negative emotions is an obstacle to navigating disarray in yourself and others.

F2: Creating effective safe spaces

A safe space is an environment where you and others feel accepted, respected, and appreciated. In times of conflict, feelings of acceptance, respect, and appreciation may become compromised. The key factor for success or failure in recovering to a safe space is allowing time to:

- Pause to see the situation from the thirtieth floor, as we discussed in Chapter One.
- Notice the misplaced need in yourself or others for self-preservation, or the desire to be right or in control.
- Slow down the urgency addiction of attempting too much too soon.
- Clarify assumptions about yourself, others, or the situation.
- Identify any unspoken expectations.
- Name the resistance to change demonstrated through discounting or grandiosity (covered in Chapter Three).

It takes a moment to zoom out to the thirtieth-floor perspective. It's a critical moment, because when you name it internally, the urge to react loses its grip on you. Even when you don't know what to do in the moment, you create space to breathe and ground yourself instead of reacting.

F3: Tailoring communication to the listener

Logically speaking, to tailor your communication to the listener, you need to understand their frame of reference, or the lens through which they see themselves, others, and the world around them. Their interpretation and the meaning they assign to what you're offering or representing is unique to them. When there's a gap in the frame of reference, it results in confusion, frustration, and possibly disappointment for all parties. To preempt a breakdown in communication, you need to:

- Clarify the meaning of your words and align your narrative with the big picture of the interaction—the purpose behind the conversation.
- Listen to the whole person, not just their words. Notice the nonverbal cues, such as their energy, tone of voice, body language, and facial expressions. Subtle mirroring would help you understand them better and respond effectively.

The three faces of waiting

Influencing outcomes requires patience and discernment—knowing when to step forward and make things happen, and when to take a step back and let things happen. You have probably found yourself struggling at times to wait for something to happen.

If you're action-driven, you may even see waiting as a temporary death or a suspension of life.

Time is a key component for the Catalyst. Just like a seed resting in the soil before sprouting or clouds gathering before the rain, life's resolutions and transformations need time to unfold. Imagine you're waiting for an opportunity and you are passing the time by:

- **Anxious waiting:** Whining and complaining all day every day that it hasn't happened yet, you're feeling more and more anxious and contaminating your social space with fear and worry. The other extreme of this is being Pollyanna-ishly optimistic, which is another form of anxiety.
- **Active waiting:** Waiting in anticipation for the moment when the opportunity comes through, trusting that even if it doesn't, you will manage and find something else that may even be better. You're paying attention to what you have at hand and getting ready for that desired moment and beyond. When you talk about what you're waiting for with others, you describe the situation using assertive words and hopeful expressions.
- **Neutral waiting:** Managing to get yourself to a neutral state, thinking that you will cross that

bridge when you reach it. Until then, you take care of your business in the best way you can.

How you wait influences the outcome of what you're waiting for and how you engage with your social space. Anxious waiting drains your time and energy, and the time and energy of those around you.

With active waiting, you gain a clear mind and a high spirit. At best, you are fully prepared to take on the opportunity and celebrate the outcome, and at worst, you are able to move forward with ease and grace.

Neutral waiting is a good fallback option when intensity is high and it's difficult to maintain a balanced emotional response regarding the matter. This is when your thoughts are distorting your feelings, so you consciously decide to park them and go about your day-to-day life as events unfold, until you gain clarity on what's next.

The Way of the Catalyst is to develop your own and others' awareness, so that you can navigate toward a state of harmony and balance. Catalysts operate from an "I'm OK, You're OK" place to create a safe space for themselves and others.

You can engage others through the power of your presence, aligned with integrity in your thoughts, words, and actions. You can inspire growth and foster collaboration in your social space. Catalysts are patient and tolerant. They are comfortable slowing down, taking time out, clarifying assumptions, managing expectations, having difficult conversations, setting boundaries, asking for help, and even taking unpopular decisions from the broader perspective of their principles, ethics, and long-term vision.

Influence is a two-way street. It is relational by nature. Every life you touch touches you back. When you make a meaningful impact on others, it changes them in some way, from the inside out. At the same time, it opens up new layers of meaning that enrich your life and deepen your alignment with the collective. This flow of Influence elevates both you and those you engage with.

Influence: Proficiency level 5

What it usually sounds like:

- Through kindness, responsible involvement or inclusion, and clarity comes cooperation.
- Everybody has the intent to cooperate, and I need to find a way to engage them first.
- I am able to manage my emotions and navigate other people's emotions without getting in the way of progress.

- People cooperate with me not because of fear, threats, or money, but because I build relationships based on fairness, honesty, and being consistent.
- I ask for opinions and perspectives as a way to move forward, not to cause delays.
- I convey harmony in my tone of voice, words, and actions; this builds trust and creates a safe space for people. This works for me, too, and I am able to ask for it when I work with others.

F1: Navigating disarray in oneself and others

The consistent ability to recognize when one or others are not aligned with The Big Picture Personal/ Collective Canvas and to take mindful actions to navigate back to it, while being gentle and compassionate with oneself and others in the process.

What it usually sounds like:

- I understand that people behave differently based on their own perceptions and experiences, and I don't take it personally.
- I am aware of things in me that might not work well for others. I navigate this in myself first, so that others don't have to deal with it.

- I am instantly aware of toxic behaviors as they emerge and am able to skillfully navigate them with myself and others.
- I ask questions to seek perspectives and understand the context before I form an opinion.
- When I am confronted about my way of thinking or doing, I am able to put my ego aside and examine the conversation in light of how what I said or did was perceived.
- Consistency is important to build trust. I am able to manage myself during the most difficult of circumstances.
- I share information openly and confront bad behavior immediately from a point of compassion, kindness, and genuinely wanting to help another person become self-aware. When I do this, people trust me as I have no agenda or ulterior motive.
- When things don't go as planned, I am able to show constructive empathy in confronting failure on my part or that of others.

F2: Creating effective safe spaces

The consistent ability to facilitate the creation of space that is safe for all, in every sense of the word, to allow for creative growth, staying mindful of the Big Picture Personal/Collective Canvas.

What it usually sounds like:

- I am able to earn cooperation and consensus with others by sharing information or expertise, working together, and putting collective success ahead of personal goals.
- In times of crisis, I am able to establish a direction for myself, making me a natural catalyst that others gravitate to.
- I am able to recognize the concerns or challenges of others, even if they are not openly expressed, for whatever reason. I create an opportunity for them to be expressed.
- I am able to recognize that ideas can also come from those who are unable or hesitant to express their points of view. I help create an opportunity to make that happen.
- During conflicts, I take the initiative to resolve confrontations and disagreements constructively, while ensuring that I treat everyone with dignity and respect.
- I ensure that I acknowledge other people's contributions openly and that the right people are credited for their efforts.
- Others see me as a source of positive influence, and they actively support each other as a result of the positive culture this inspires.

F3: Tailoring communication to the listener

The consistent ability to actively listen and articulate in a way that complements and aligns with the other's tone, pace, energy, words, emotions, and expressions, where the focus is on the Big Picture Personal/Collective Canvas.

What it usually sounds like:

- I know how words and tone can make or break outcomes when communicating.
- I am able to engage people within their frame of reference and use words based on how they perceive them. I don't waste time clarifying because I can avoid ambiguity the first time around.
- I am not confined to one specific style or tone. I bring conversations to life and make them engaging and enriching in a variety of ways.
- It is important to engage the hearts and minds of the people I am interacting with, especially when it matters.
- I make sure I am prepared for interactions, and I keep them simple, clear, and to the point, without extra elements that can cause confusion or ambiguity.
- I am consistent in formal and informal situations.

- I am able to leverage the intelligence and experience of the people I am interacting with.
- Bringing together harmony in tone of voice, words, and actions is important to build trust and create safe spaces for people.
- I am always aware that what I think, say, and do has an impact on myself and others.
- My language is positive, uplifting, forward-looking, and gets to the point.

Key points

- Influence: Causing an effect without force:
  - F1: Navigating disarray in oneself and others.
  - F2: Creating effective safe spaces.
  - F3: Tailoring communication to the listener.
- Force, used mindfully and purposefully, is a great approach to manage emergencies, disrupt toxic patterns, and enforce order and structure in chaotic situations.
- Relying on force alone sacrifices trust and long-term constructive impact.
- Influence requires empathy, presence, and clarity. It's about igniting momentum, adding meaning, and inspiring a shift in perspective.

- OKness means holding yourself and others as worthy, resourceful, and whole.
- The "I'm OK, You're OK" stance frees you from counterproductive excuses that you might otherwise make for yourself or others.
- Tolerance is dysfunctional when it enables harmful behavior and suppresses change.
- Benign tolerance aligns with the big picture and permits sustainability, nurture, connection, growth, and progress without compromising principles or well-being.
- A moment of reflection from a higher perspective helps create a space between you and your thoughts, feelings, and the situation at hand. That space brings clarity and alignment with your big picture.
- Understanding others' frames of reference allows you to communicate with clarity and avoid any confusion, frustration, or disappointment.

7

Excellence: Bringing The Dynamic Self, Moment To Moment

The dynamic self is the part of you that is alive, evolving, and responsive to life as it unfolds. It is neither bound by past experiences nor limited by present challenges. Unattached to roles, titles, status, or achievements, the dynamic self moves freely, guided not by a fixed identity, but by presence and alignment with the big picture. It is agile and aware, able to tune in to both the inner world and the environment around it. It zooms in and out with ease, perceiving life from both the ground level and the wide-angle view from the thirtieth floor. It stays engaged in the unfolding of life's process and flows with change, rather than resisting it.

The attitude of Excellence is not something you switch on when luck is on your side, or when life is neatly falling into place. It isn't measured solely by the quality of your work or how well things turn out. Through the lens of the Catalyst, Excellence is a way of being, especially in moments of uncertainty, pressure, or disruption. It reveals itself in your attitude when things don't go according to plan, in how you bounce back after a setback, and in the inner strength you draw on when the way forward is unclear.

In such moments, you need your dynamic self to lead the way—not the one that clings to certainty and rushes to escape the discomfort of the moment, but the one that listens, adjusts, and responds with courage and integrity. Excellence lives in your ability to stay responsive and real, even when the path ahead is unclear, the light at the end of the tunnel has yet to appear, or you're unsure if the tunnel has an end at all.

Three traits of Excellence

Excellence is often mistaken for perfection, performance, or achievement. But for the Catalyst, Excellence is not a fixed standard; it's an attitude. It is the fifth attitude of the Catalyst and can be recognized in the way you navigate your life, measured by three defining traits:

- X1: Self-worth anchored in responsiveness to change
- X2: Direction inspired by the big picture
- X3: Courage in action

Between the familiar and the unknown lies a liminal space, a threshold that is often raw, quiet, and deeply uncomfortable. It's a space where the old self loses its grip, but the new self hasn't yet emerged. Often there's an urge to rush through this space, seeking certainty before it's ready to be revealed. But if you can stay there just long enough, without forcing clarity or escaping the discomfort, something extraordinary happens. You create room for possibilities, reinventions, and breakthroughs beyond what you once believed possible.

Remaining steady in the liminal space needs more than patience. It requires alignment with your unshakable essence, the part of you that no circumstance can take away—your self-worth anchored in your responsiveness to change (X1). It calls for clarity on your big picture and the direction you choose, even when the path ahead is not yet clear (X2). And it rests on your courage to take timely action even when the outcome is not guaranteed (X3). In other words, it requires you to bring your dynamic self, moment to moment.

From heart attack to living a dream: What the system couldn't take away

I am sharing my father's story as an example of Excellence. His name is Amin, which means "the keeper of trust" in Arabic. He continues to live up to that name every day. He has faced less-than-fortunate circumstances. Instead of letting them define him, he redefined his big picture, accounting for the reality of a corrupt system that prioritized obedience and political allegiance over qualifications and talent.

Amin received his high school diploma in 1966. Like many young men of his generation, he was eager to work and carve out a meaningful place in society. His first opportunity came in 1967 in the field of journalism and media. This early taste of career momentum was interrupted less than a year later when he was called to fulfill almost four years of mandatory military service.

Those years were a test of endurance, a period marked by relentless hardship and no significant achievement beyond serving that national duty. It was a time when he had no choice but to embrace reality as it unfolded, focusing on one day at a time and carrying out his duties with discipline, while longing for the scent of home and the familiar sounds of the neighborhood where he grew up.

After completing his military service, he returned to civilian life with renewed determination. His focus shifted from mere survival to creating something of worth. He enrolled in journalism studies and graduated with distinction. Around this time, he met and married my mother, a certified elementary school teacher who was full of energy and carried herself with unwavering resolve. Together, they began to build a shared future grounded in stability, learning, and mutual support.

Their life was far from simple. They faced financial uncertainty, limited resources, and the arrival of their first child, my elder brother, within a short time. They leaned into the chaos with the long view in mind. Both pursued university degrees, despite the mounting responsibilities of parenthood and work. Their purpose was to support their children's future and carry themselves through the uncertainties of aging with dignity.

Amin's genius found its expression in the written word. With talent, integrity, and persistence, he advanced rapidly through the professional ranks to lead the foreign news division at the Syrian Arab News Agency (SANA). He was also elected as an independent member of the Executive Office of the Journalist's Union, a special achievement made possible by having his colleagues' trust and a clean record, despite the political restrictions and suppression of freedoms in the country.

However, none of these accomplishments earned him favor with the ruling authorities, as he refused to become a member of the Ba'ath Party. He was denied the privileges that his party-affiliated peers enjoyed, including the valuable opportunity of being sent abroad as an overseas correspondent for SANA. It was a chance that could have transformed his life on many levels, but for him, no achievement was worth trading his integrity. That was simply non-negotiable.

He later survived two heart attacks, just one year apart. The second awakened him to a sobering truth: his once-held dream of leaving a mark on the world through his writing was unlikely to come true in the way he imagined. He decided to shift the dream and find a new meaning for his life, away from the world of media and journalism.

He created a new vision for the future, defined by peace, health, and connection. He imagined a life amid nature, far from the noise and pollution of the city, where he and my mother could be healthy, happy, and part of a community that surrounds them with joy and warmth. That's exactly what they built. Over the years, they cared for their physical health through daily walks, a balanced diet, and regular checkups. They kept their brains active with learning, reading, and expanding their knowledge. They nurtured a vibrant social circle that brought joy and vitality. They were both at peace from having held their moral compass sacred above all else. To this day, they stand as a living example of alignment, clarity, and courage.

They made a beautiful home in the Syrian mountains, overlooking the sea, surrounded by a rich land where they grew flowers, fruits, and vegetables. The area where they live is a hub for thinkers, writers, artists, and musicians who draw inspiration from the breathtaking views and the crisp, clean air infused with the scent of nature. Soon after they moved, their home became a gathering place for the local creative community where they share laughter, meals, music, and deep conversations.

Let's examine the story through the eyes of the Catalyst. What truly stands out in Amin's story is not a single dramatic turning point or grand moment, but a steady series of intentional choices, moment by moment.

Being blocked by systemic injustice despite his talent and dedication took its toll, but it didn't stop him. His self-worth was not tied to external factors like status, wealth, or titles. Instead, he placed his faith in himself and his ability to adjust course while remaining true to his principles. He made decisions that he respected and stood by in the long run. That, more than anything, was his source of inner strength and comfort.

His choices—returning to study, building a career, securing the family future, redefining his dream, and building a community—were never reactions to pressure. They were guided by a living and dynamic big picture that he drew for himself. He found his way to a healthy and fulfilling life, overcoming all the obstacles that stood in his way.

Apart from declining political alignment, Amin's courage manifested in rebuilding his life multiple times. In his eighties now, his mind is sharp as a tack, and his eloquence appears boundless. He is physically fit and full of energy, with a piquant wit. People around him love and respect him greatly. No system could take his determination to stay true to himself, to make the best of what life had to offer, and to turn his vision into a lived experience.

The process of learning, relearning, and unlearning

As the dynamic self lies at the heart of Excellence, Excellence itself is not a fixed state that you automatically stay in once reached. It's an ongoing, ever-expanding attitude. It calls for learning, relearning, and unlearning worn-out habits and beliefs to sustain alignment with yourself, clarity on your direction, and courage to take the road less travelled.

Learning is often associated with formal education or school days, which do not typically go beyond acquiring knowledge, understanding required concepts and theories, and memorizing formulas, facts, or texts to pass exams. That knowledge is hardly retained or internalized to shape our thinking or way of living.

The learning for Excellence is the kind of learning that grows you, enhances your life, and reshapes your thinking and behavior to achieve intentional results. This is a learning that you choose based on what is important to help you live the big picture of your life here and now. Your life is not the projection of your Big Picture Personal Canvas, but rather the projector.

This kind of learning might not get you a medal or any formal recognition, but it will have a lasting impact on your life and your character. Learning for life opens up your curiosity, imagination, and endless possibilities. It is available everywhere through studying a subject, reading a book, listening to a podcast, observing your surroundings, examining your experiences, watching a movie, or listening to a story. Once you open yourself up to life learning, you will find constant inspiration all around. It then becomes possible to take that little piece of learning and allow it to change you in some way. If you consistently grow in this way, imagine your sense of liberation from old patterns and limiting beliefs within a year—truly remarkable. Wouldn't such an ability become a reason to love yourself even more?

Since a very early age, every time we watched a movie, Amin used to ask me, "What do you think is the message from this movie?" For him, nothing was too small to derive a life lesson from. That was fun learning, effortlessly integrated into my being as a child.

When I asked dozens of people what they would do with their life if they lived for 500 years, didn't age, were fit and healthy, and had no financial worries, everyone responded with a desire to learn or share their learning in some way. Things like traveling, exploring different cultures, playing musical instruments, developing skills or talents, competing in sports, becoming a public speaker, inventing a new technology, or learning new languages. This reveals that learning is not something that prepares us for life; it is the expression of life itself and of being alive.

Relearning is revisiting what you already know with a deeper understanding and expanded perspective within a new context or experience. This is when your new level of awareness brings a new meaning to a value that matters to you. For example, when the trust that you used to place in others becomes an ability to trust yourself in any relationship or situation. Independence grows from being self-sufficient to being autonomous. Success expands from a one-dimensional measure of work or study to include all areas of your life, both personal and professional.

Unlearning is identifying and letting go of the beliefs, habits, practices, and attachments that no longer serve you. Just as nature doesn't allow a vacuum, unlearning must be followed by intentionally integrating something new to take the place of what you let go. Embracing a new pattern cannot survive in isolation; it requires realignment of other areas in your life to support the change and sustain progress. For example, suppose you're releasing your people-pleasing tendency and replacing it with a new habit of setting boundaries and asking for what you need. In that case, you need to support that shift by redefining your self-worth, reevaluating certain relationships, and learning how to communicate to make yourself heard.

Learning for life involves an ongoing interplay between learning, relearning, and unlearning—a continuous process of updating and upgrading your thinking, attitudes, and behaviors, to enhance your dynamic self. It's not a linear path that always moves forward. It also moves inward and backward through reflection, revisiting, and sometimes letting go, allowing you to expand, stay grounded, and free yourself from what no longer serves you in order to embrace what does.

Responsiveness: The active participation in life's unfolding

If learning for life is the turbo of the dynamic self, responsiveness is its expression. Responsiveness means engaging in your life experience and relationships with presence, intent, and clarity. This manifests through active listening, asking for help, sharing your perspective in an unattached manner, articulating your thoughts or feelings in a non-judgmental way, setting boundaries, gaining closure on a relationship or a phase of your life, taking initiative, making a request, facing a challenge, or leading a difficult conversation.

Being responsive does not mean having it all figured out; it simply means stepping out of the bystander position. In that role, the easy option is to remain passive due to fear of getting it wrong, confusion about who you are and what you need, being limited by old ways of thinking and action, wishing to avoid conflict, or feeling hopeless about change and terrified of the transitional phase it requires. It's like sitting on the sidelines in your own game instead of being on the field playing your part.

The story of Randy Pausch, a professor of computer science at Carnegie Mellon University in Pittsburgh, USA, and father of three children, touched hearts as a powerful example of responsiveness at its highest level.

Randy was in his mid-forties when he was diagnosed with cancer in September 2006. In August 2007, he was told that he had between three and six months of good health left. One month after he got his terminal diagnosis, he gave a talk titled "The Last Lecture".[18] He appeared on stage with energy and a beautiful, big smile, sprinkling in jokes. He started his lecture by addressing the "elephant in the room" of his health condition using CAT scan images to show approximately ten tumors on his liver, before he said:

> "That is what it is; we can't change it. We just have to decide how we're going to respond to that. We cannot change the cards we are dealt, just how we play the hand. If I don't seem as

> depressed or morose as I should be, sorry to disappoint you."

His lecture wasn't about death, it was about how to live. He talked about his childhood dreams, enabling the dreams of others, and the lessons he had learned. He ended the lecture by saying, "It's not about how to achieve your dreams; it's about how you lead your life. If you lead your life the right way, the karma will take care of itself, the dreams will come to you." The talk went viral and was turned into a bestselling book, *The Last Lecture.*[19]

Randy chose to remain responsive, even in the face of the sobering reality of his diagnosis. He didn't spend his final months chasing more time or sinking into despair. Instead, he focused on leaving a legacy for his children, students, and the world, while arranging the logistics for after he was gone for his family and embracing every moment he had left with them.

There is power and transcendent joy in actively participating in the unfolding of your life, because you were never meant to be a bystander. You don't need the certainty of having everything figured out right away. You don't need to be fearless; courage is about accepting fear and doing it anyway. And you don't need to feel powerful; your vulnerability is enough to begin. Responsiveness is your willingness to meet life where it is, embodying the right attitudes to shape your journey and impact the world around you.

Excellence: Proficiency level 5

What it usually sounds like:

- My definition of success has evolved beyond material possessions and achievements. I seek a deeper understanding of myself as I move forward.
- I am able to set aside time for what really matters in the long run and to say "no" without hesitation if it would take me away from the big picture.
- I am able to maintain respectful boundaries with those around me.
- I am able to balance my personal needs with the needs of others without making any unnecessary compromises.
- I can empathize with the struggles and intentions of others and make allowances when needed.
- My sense of purpose from the big picture I made for myself gives me guidance, comfort, and strength. It gives me clarity when things are ambiguous.
- I don't make promises. I say what I do and do what I say.
- Whether it is short-term or long-term gain, I am able to ensure that what I do today always aligns with the big picture.
- Each day is a smaller version of the life I have chosen for myself.

- My self-talk is positive, encouraging, and progressive.

X1: Self-worth anchored in responsiveness to change

The consistent ability to draw guidance, security, comfort, and hope from the Big Picture Personal Canvas as the source of inner strength that makes one a catalyst or driver for change for the purpose of growth and renewal.

What it usually sounds like:

- I have evolved beyond "people and things" to be my own source of strength.
- I am able to lean on others for support when needed without shame or guilt.
- I appreciate worldly things without my identity being defined by them.
- I am aware of when I can contribute and when I can't. I am able to step aside to make way for someone who can.
- I am able to set firm, respectful boundaries for myself as well as others.
- I embody the phrase, "It is not what happened, but rather how we respond that matters."
- I can balance my needs with the needs of others.

- I am able to see elements of myself in others, with all the struggles and glory, and it makes me respectful of all.
- I handle criticism well. I am able to focus on the core message without getting distracted, distanced, or diverted by the delivery of criticism.
- If my contributions are not mentioned, it does not make me insecure or bitter. My internal compass determines if I have added value or not, and this recognition gives me momentum.

X2: Direction inspired by the big picture

The consistent ability to make each moment a version of the Big Picture Personal Canvas and channel the complete self (stories, emotions, energies, beliefs, and actions) into it.

What it usually sounds like:

- My personal vision of continuous improvement is always at the forefront of my thoughts and conduct.
- Each day is a scaled-down, smaller version of the life I desire for myself. I run my life in a calm, kind manner, not driven by an urgency addiction.
- I understand that life can be unpredictable despite my best efforts to control and predict it. I can control the way I process and respond to it.

- I have no hesitation in saying "no" if the request doesn't add value or if the person asking for help could manage on their own with a gentle nudge.
- I make sure my thoughts, words, and actions are aligned with meaningful outcomes for myself and the people around me.
- I can thrive in chaos, and I am not threatened by ambiguity. In stressful times, I am even calmer and clearer. I am able to detach myself, find balance, and resume the process.
- While I experience a range of emotions and feelings, I am able to put them into perspective and focus on the larger purpose.
- I am able to stay oriented in the present and determine what serves my vision, what doesn't, the likely setbacks, and the potential solutions. I do this with peace, collaboration, and firmness of purpose. I accept that challenges are a fundamental part of the journey.
- I am happy to navigate life and, where necessary, acquire skills, share, and delegate. I use my energy efficiently and recover gracefully from setbacks.
- I like to stay ahead of myself, paying attention to both the means and the end, so that they are in harmony, sustainable, and renewable. The journey and the destination are equally important.

X3: Courage in action

The consistent ability to demonstrate courage in the face of change and uncertainty, while living a life rich with purpose, making it easy and gentle for others, and sharing and receiving from a place of abundance.

What it usually sounds like:

- I pay close attention to what needs to be done and how it needs to be done. There is little or no gap between intent, execution, and outcome.
- I trust myself, and I trust in how life will evolve. My acceptance of ambiguity helps me make decisions and take actions that others call inspiring and courageous. It's a way of life for me.
- I am able to adapt my thoughts, feelings, and actions, select resources, and execute in a manner that matches the needs of the moment while focusing on the ultimate result. This has come with a lot of practice and by learning from errors over time.
- Irrespective of how easy or difficult the circumstances are, I know I need to stay light, balanced, and true to my principles no matter what changes around me.
- I hold myself accountable for my thoughts, words, and actions. I hold other people accountable for their own.

- I show up prepared all the time.
- I hold myself to a high standard and invite others to do the same for themselves.
- I don't judge people. Everybody has some reason for what they do. I operate from a place of empathy and compassion when people around me falter or struggle to stay true to their words and actions.
- I am aware that I have the freedom to choose my response in any situation. The big picture guides me.
- People enjoy my company and find it uplifting, calming, and inspiring.

Key points

- Excellence: Bringing the dynamic self, moment to moment:
  - X1: Self-worth anchored in responsiveness to change.
  - X2: Direction inspired by the big picture.
  - X3: Courage in action.
- The dynamic self is the part of you that is alive, evolving, and responsive to life as it unfolds. It is unlimited and unattached.

- Excellence is a way of being, especially in moments of uncertainty, under pressure, or during times of disruption.
- The liminal space lies between the familiar and the unknown, a threshold that is often raw, quiet, and deeply uncomfortable. To remain steady in the liminal space, you need self-worth anchored in your responsiveness to change, direction guided by your big picture, and courage to take timely action.
- Learning, relearning, and unlearning intertwine to update and upgrade your thinking, actions, and behavior, enhancing your dynamic self.
- Responsiveness means engaging in your life experience and relationships with presence, intent, and clarity. It is meeting life where it is and embodying the right attitudes to shape your journey and impact the world around you.

PART THREE

LIVING THE WAY OF THE CATALYST

Up to this point, you've explored the catalyst fundamentals of answering the call for change and the Big Picture Personal Canvas. You've also walked through the Five Attitudes of the Catalyst, seeing them not just as ideas, but as inner capacities that shape your life experience.

Now, in Part Three, we will discover how the concept of the Catalyst is lived in its entirety.

This section explores the lives of two individuals—Zimmy and Michel—who embody the Way of the Catalyst in different ways. Their stories are not offered as perfect examples, but as real and resonant illustrations of what it looks like when the catalytic attitudes come to life. You'll see moments of choice, clarity, courage, and connection, all expressed in the natural rhythm of their journeys.

Zimmy's path begins in personal transformation. Her story reveals how the Catalyst's power emerges when the heart is open, the head is clear, and life is lived moment to moment, from the inside out. Through deep self-awareness, intuitive resilience, and an unwavering trust in her inner compass, she created ripples that now touch the lives of children, families, and communities.

Michel's path unfolds in the high-stakes world of corporate leadership. Faced with difficult decisions, conflicting expectations, and the emotional weight of large-scale change, he shows how catalytic leadership can balance humanity with strategy. His story highlights the attitudes in action when under pressure—authority without control, clarity with empathy, and consistency over perfection.

You'll notice that both Zimmy and Michel navigated their journeys with grace, not because life was easy, but because they engaged with it consciously. Let their stories inspire you.

The final chapter, Becoming The Catalyst, invites you to reflect on your own life and leadership. You don't need to wait for a title, role, or turning point. This chapter will help you begin living from the inside out, intentionally, courageously, and in alignment with your principles, becoming the Catalyst you were born to be.

8

Zimmy: The Catalyst Next Door

Catalysts are all around us. They stand out to us because of the meaningful impact they make on our lives. What sets them apart is how they continue to show up, even during times of adversity in their own lives. They preserve their integrity under pressure, without getting consumed in the process. They bring power, clarity, and courage; their presence inspires us, and they make things easier and simpler in the most graceful and delightful ways.

When I began reflecting on people around me who truly embody the attitudes and traits described in this book, one name rose to the surface without hesitation: Zimmy Khan.

Zimmy Khan has a PhD in clinical hypnotherapy and is a master practitioner of neurolinguistic programming (NLP) and cognitive behavioral therapy (CBT). She is also a practitioner of *Reiki,* pranic energy healing, and emotional freedom technique (EFT), a life coach, and the founder of Epiphany and The Love Academy (for nurturing little hearts) in Dubai.[20,21]

I first heard Zimmy's name in passing at a social gathering, when a woman shared how a hypnotherapy experience with Zimmy had transformed her life. I was intrigued by her story, and not long after, I booked my first session with Zimmy. That was over a decade ago. Looking back now, I often wonder at how different my life would have been if I had not made that call.

Since then, Zimmy has become so much more than a professional I turn to. She's become a dear friend and mentor, someone who has helped me open my heart, expand my awareness, and move wholeheartedly into a life of peace, ease, and joy. She has walked with me on a path of discovery and transformation and has stood as an unwavering beacon of hope and faith for a future that surpasses the past and even the present.

Zimmy's early life was anything but ordinary, filled with challenges no child should have to face. But she came through it without losing herself, radiating catalytic attitudes into the social space and touching thousands of lives throughout her journey with elegant grace and a cheeky sense of humor.

She graciously shares parts of her life story in *The Way of the Catalyst,* offering a full expression of the Five Attitudes of the Catalyst.

Zimmy's story

Zimmy was born in Karachi, Pakistan, and lost her mother when she was one and a half years old. Her father was unable to take care of her, so he put her in the care of a childless married couple who were close to them during the first year of her life. They became her foster parents, and when they relocated to Saudi Arabia, she went with them, while her biological father followed shortly after.

Zimmy reflects on her early life: "I was obviously a very small child, and I didn't have any choices, I was taken wherever. I used to be ping-ponged between two homes. Unfortunately, neither of them was a place where I felt safe or experienced a sense of belonging, affection, or genuine, unconditional love. Everything was very conditional. At that point, I was just trying to go along with and listen to everyone, to be the good child and not give anyone problems, because I didn't feel like anyone really wanted me. I felt like I was a burden that had to be taken care of, and that's why two sets of people couldn't handle me. No one really wanted me."

She continues, "Now I know that was just my interpretation as a child. That was one of the more negative perspectives that I took at that time. Once I grew up, I realized I actually had twice as many people to love and care for me, if I had chosen to see that."

As she grew older, her expanding awareness helped her reframe emotionally charged situations. For example, when her father gave her a hard time for not visiting him on the weekends, she chose to see it through a higher lens—understanding that beneath his complaints was a desire to have her close. Since he had been harsh with her as a child, his approach felt like emotional blackmail. Over time, she came to realize that it was simply his unorthodox and unpolished way of expressing that he wanted her in his life.

Growing up in Saudi Arabia came with certain restrictions. She didn't have much of a choice when it came to playmates, seeing only the children of family friends. The only place where Zimmy felt safe was at school, because there she had a tiny sense of freedom and different children to play with. In the 1970s, there was little awareness of autism and dyslexia and how they affected children. Zimmy had both and felt the need to pretend to be "normal" to fit in, even though nothing in her life was truly normal.

She said, "I used to try to pretend, because that was safer, and it created a sense of belonging which is what I always wanted in my life—the basics which a lot of kids take for granted."

As a child, Zimmy was reserved and quiet. She learned to be self-sufficient from an early age. She didn't need prompting or encouragement, or for life to have some sense of normalcy, for her to do her part. She used to finish her homework without reminders and clean her room herself. She had a few friends, not necessarily by choice, but because they took her in and accepted her. She nurtured those relationships. As a coping mechanism, she dealt with many things with humor and sarcasm. Making people laugh gave her great satisfaction, and to this day, she enjoys a hearty laugh.

Zimmy explains, "As a child, I was very alone. I used to sleep to escape. Whenever I got overwhelmed, I would sleep for hours. Sensory overload, for an autistic person, often means that even everyday stimuli can become too much to handle.

"My foster father had his own challenges to deal with. One minute, we would be laughing after I cracked a joke. Suddenly, one wrong word that he took personally, and everything would change. We could go from laughing hysterically to a complete blowup so quickly that I was walking on eggshells around him most of the time.

"My foster mother didn't warm up to me either, and dealing with all of that as a three-year-old took its toll. In retrospect, I can see people for who they are today. Everyone had their baggage, their issues, their insecurities, and I've made peace with all of it. It was hard, but I made it through."

Between autism, dyslexia, and the transition to adolescence, every experience was amplified and heavy. There were even times when Zimmy had suicidal thoughts. She identified a building near her house that was fifteen stories tall. Every morning, she would wake up, look out of the window, and tell herself, "If today becomes too hard, we can go there and jump off. No worries, no problem, just do today."

Although there was a darkness to it, she realizes now that her self-talk about being present and in the moment was akin to doing therapy for herself, before she knew what therapy was. She was "parenting herself."

Zimmy says, "The adult voice inside me was thankfully very mature, kind, and practical. For example, I was told that I was ugly, and that was why my mom had left me and my dad didn't want me. Imagine what a harsh thing that is for a child to hear. My inner voice never used to tell me, 'You're beautiful, everyone is lying,' but rather it used to show me things like a woman in the newspaper who won an award for peace for doing something great. She was not beautiful—she was quite ordinary to look at—but, 'Look at her,' the voice would say, 'she's done a great job!'

"Then we—me and my guiding inner voice—would go to the matrimonial section of the paper and see 'not-so-attractive' people getting married. 'Oh, so it's OK if I'm not beautiful, or even if I'm ugly. I can see many ordinary-looking people doing great things.

Actually, most of the well-known people who made the newspaper headlines are not attractive.' So, I used to tell myself, 'Don't worry about it!'

"My inner voice was very practical. It used to tell me, 'Just do your best. Do what you can to make yourself look OK, but don't worry about it.' It was very kind in the sense that I didn't delude myself, but also I didn't let myself fall into the trap. That helped me. So, in my teenage years, I did the best I could every day. Then, at the end of the day, I would assess, 'How was it on a scale of ten? Seven—not bad at all! That's OK, we can handle this. Let's do it again tomorrow.' I literally kept myself alive through the darkest times by ticking off one day at a time, which is apparently a great practice that we prescribe to people nowadays."

The intuitive wisdom of Zimmy's younger self helped her make sense of things in her own way. She came to see that the hurtful things people around her said or did were simply reflections of their own way of expressing themselves. She didn't let those things define her. Instead, she tuned in to the steady inner voice of truth, which never failed her. Any other approach might have pulled her into a downward spiral, leading her to lose herself.

Zimmy's courage and self-sufficiency empowered her to make decisions that weren't always popular and to own them fully. For example, when her father offered to take her to the United States to obtain citizenship, an opportunity that could have significantly changed her life, she chose not to go. It was a good opportunity, but it didn't feel right in her heart. Instead, she honored her own design for her life and didn't settle for what was offered.

She decided to come to Dubai in 1997 to pursue a university degree and live independently. She landed a job even before graduating, thrived in her career, and in 2008—in the middle of the recession—she left the corporate world, trusting it was the right next step. She eventually discovered a new path in hypnotherapy, to which she committed fully. And she made it happen. As she put it, "It was my faith in following my heart rather than working very hard."

Even then, she had to live one day at a time to make it through: "I'm in my fifties, and if there's anything that I can do today, if there's anything that I can experience this month, or if there's anything that I can create, I aim to do it now. I don't know about the future."

Every year on her birthday, she sits down with her inner friend and says, "You know, we just completed another year. Let's say we get one more—what do we want to do during this year?" When she has an urge, a passion, or a feeling of excitement about something, she gives it her best shot.

Zimmy doesn't take herself too seriously, nor does she aim for perfection. She believes that when an outcome meets her own standards, it will be good enough by many standards because, she says, "I respect myself. It's not about chasing perfection, which can be elusive, but about doing what's possible now."

Zimmy's alignment, clarity, and courage allow both her personal and professional life to flow with ease and grace. She responds to opportunities that call her, gives them her best, and lives them fully. Something always opens up, and she keeps going, trusting that life has got her back.

Despite the challenges of neurodivergence and the complexity of her family dynamics, Zimmy managed to create a safe space for herself. She influenced herself in powerful ways, and later, as an adult, she extended that influence to others. Instead of wasting precious time and energy searching for flaws within herself, she chose to reframe the negative messages from her environment and allow herself to connect with inner harmony and peace. She would tell herself, "That's not a flaw; if I use it like this, it's a strength." Take stubbornness, for example. She would think, "If I become stubborn about taking care of myself, that's actually a really good thing."

Zimmy approached life with the belief that we are each made in a certain way, and nothing is perfect. But we can make something deeply meaningful out of it when we align with our inner source of wisdom and strength. At a professional level, Zimmy's experience helped her see without a shadow of doubt that we all have that inner source of wisdom and strength. She feels proud of herself, but she doesn't feel superior in any way.

Zimmy invests her time and energy in short-term visions that, together, shape a uniquely intentional and proactive way of living. Present and grounded in the moment, her self-worth is anchored not only in her ability to adapt to change, but also in her willingness to create it when needed, fully trusting in her own contribution and in the contributions of those around her.

Zimmy's method is simple: she identifies what she wants, breaks it down into small, actionable steps, and engages dedicated people like her to add value to the world, focusing on what can be done now rather than getting lost in what might happen tomorrow. That's how she brought The Love Academy to life in 2019, a clear example of Interdependence in action.[22] The Love Academy is a non-profit initiative dedicated to nurturing the emotional well-being of children worldwide. Drawing from her own challenging childhood and decades of therapeutic experience, Zimmy developed a heart-centered curriculum designed to help children access their innate "superpowers"—like love, kindness, gratitude, and self-worth.

"I see people constantly seeking external validation and guidance," she said. "My mission, for as long as I'm here, is to give people back to themselves. Growing up, many of us lose our spark—that essence that reminds us we're here to do something revolutionary for ourselves, in our own little universe. To become the best version of ourselves. It doesn't have to be big. It just has to be true. Sometimes, the search for what's missing within can take a lifetime. In my work, this is my focus: to help as many people as possible reconnect with their inner source of trust and knowing, to rely on themselves."

In her personal life, Zimmy says she was a very different person until around the age of thirty: "At that point, I still wasn't aware. I was still learning how to keep myself safe and nurture myself. My focus was very much on me—survival, healing, finding stability. That self-focus created a sense of separation between me and others.

"I used to envy people who seemed to have easier lives. They looked so light, relaxed, and positive, and I didn't feel any of that. I was quite negative, always anxious, always worrying that something would go wrong. I was also very cynical. I didn't trust people. I judged them.

"But all of that was just my way of trying to protect myself, to carve out the space I needed to heal. Once that inner work reached a point where I could say I truly loved myself unconditionally, things started to shift—I started noticing kindness, good things were happening, and I met people who helped restore my faith in humanity.

"It's been a journey from age thirty to fifty, and I've become someone who now sees the goodness in everyone. Even when someone isn't acting their best, I can see they've likely been hurt in some way. That alone calls for love and compassion. My perspective has shifted 180°. Now I assume that people can be trusted until they show me otherwise. I assume the world is a safe place. I assume life has my back and always has. I've gathered enough evidence to believe that. Yes, I'm intuitive, but I'm also analytical. When anxiety shows up, I remind myself, 'Look at your track record. Things have always worked out. No point worrying. Just do your best. Even if things go wrong, there will be solutions, it's OK.'

"I don't feel alone anymore. I don't feel unsafe. I don't feel like running away. I sleep less, and I feel more connected. I'm honored to be here. I'm glad I stayed. And for as long as I am here, I will keep being kind. Kinder than I ever thought I could be. Everything is an experience. It passes. Then, I'm back in my head, having conversations with my inner self, asking, 'Why did I feel that? Can I feel better? Can I look at this differently?' That's just how I live now."

People are sometimes skeptical of her kindness at first. Zimmy says, "I think some people aren't used to genuine kindness or acceptance. There's often an inner debate—'Is she fake? Is this too much? That's weird!'—but eventually, they come around, and I can feel the shift. They become more open and accepting.

"I tell people, 'I love you,' and they don't always say it back right away. Sometimes it's just 'right back at you,' and that's fine. I don't need to hear it back—I love myself enough, and I have enough love in my life. But over time, they start saying it, and I go, 'Ah, thank you. You're opening your heart!'

"I think we all need to open our hearts, and that's what I want to see more of. I try to encourage it, not by forcing it, but by being it. I've been on the other side, when my heart was closed and my life felt small and full of fear. Now I live differently, and I want others to feel that too. Everyone deserves this."

The journey is not always smooth and joyful. Challenges inevitably arise. Sometimes, the challenge takes the form of a person with whom we must interact, even when it drains our energy.

Zimmy says, "Unless there's a direct attack on you, don't take it personally. It turns out to be the wise choice 90% of the time. It's really about how we perceive the so-called 'difficult person.' If we stay relaxed, we start to see more clearly. It often turns out that we are judging them because they are in a place we were in before, and we are actually judging ourselves. Or they are people that we aspire to be and we envy them, whether consciously or unconsciously.

"We're all on a journey, after all. Let people process their stuff in their own time. And in 10% of cases, where there is a direct personal attack, you stand up for yourself. You don't need to stoop to their level. Stay calm and firmly ask for what you need. Don't be mean or harsh beyond what's necessary. Sometimes, that's all it takes.

"There are people who act mean or nasty simply because no one has ever stood up to them. A couple of people in my life were bullies. I found that if you fight them, it becomes a competition. But when you hold yourself steady and draw the line clearly and firmly, that's usually enough. It's not a debate. It's not a confrontation. It's just a boundary, and most of the time, it works."

Zimmy has made life easy for herself and those around her by embodying the Five Attitudes of the Catalyst. She is peaceful and cheerful, and it's contagious. People around her seem to absorb her serenity and joyfulness by osmosis. As a Catalyst, Zimmy's big picture is not a distant future fantasy or deathbed wish—it's here and now. She is the living projector of her own Big Picture Personal Canvas, expressed moment to moment.

Moving forward, Zimmy simply wants more of the same. She believes there's still much to do, in exactly the same way. She said, "I don't have any huge plans, but I want to do more with The Love Academy. I want to spread our heart-based syllabus to underprivileged children and into more mainstream schools, to make sure we give our children, our future generation, the tools we didn't have and are now learning.

"If we give children those tools early in life, their most productive years can be truly amazing, because they'll be creating rather than reacting. We've spent so long reacting to life, then trying to fix the things we created by default. I want to give children what they deserve—more time. I want them to deal less with baggage and emotional heaviness and instead be present and create the kind of world we all want for them. That's the part that will continue, and I'll be focusing on it more and more.

"I love what I do, and I know that for now, it's my purpose—I'm on plan. On a personal level, I want to play more. I'm now giving my inner child the chance to really be a child. So, I want to play, travel, relax, enjoy, and be silly, because I deserve it. I've already surpassed most of my plans and expectations for myself. There's no pressure now to do anything more."

Zimmy's way: A catalytic lens

Zimmy lives the Five Attitudes of the Catalyst in a way that seems seamless, almost instinctive. But make no mistake, her ease didn't come without effort. It's the result of deep personal work, conscious choice, and an unwavering commitment to life and growth. What's remarkable is how these attitudes don't show up in big declarations or dramatic shifts. They're woven into the everyday moments of her life—how she listens, makes decisions, and stays present in times of both ease and discomfort.

Responsibility, for Zimmy, begins within. She takes ownership of her thoughts, emotions, and the meaning she assigns to life's events. She is attuned to her emotional states and aware of how they impact her inner world and her relationships. Rather than reacting out of pain, she pauses, reflects, and responds in ways that serve the highest good of all involved. Especially when things get hard, she turns inward, listens deeply, and consciously makes life-affirming choices. This isn't about controlling every feeling; it's about staying grounded in the big picture and moving forward with clarity, inner strength, and integrity.

Her Proactivity isn't about rigid plans or ticking boxes—it's about living with intention. Zimmy doesn't drift through life on autopilot; she knows what matters to her and shapes her days around it. She is guided by an inner compass, her inner friend, that she accesses by turning her attention inward. She doesn't wait for change to happen; she meets it halfway by creating space for something new to emerge and committing herself to a path she consciously chooses, such as when she left her corporate job to pursue a path of therapy and healing. No matter how many times life tested her resolve, she kept showing up with courage, clarity, and grace.

Interdependence may be where Zimmy's light shines most naturally. She embodies a special blend of humility and self-assuredness, grounded in her own value while being deeply respectful of others. She knows how to ask for help without shrinking and how to offer support without overpowering. She collaborates with others from a place of resourcefulness and wholeness, rather than neediness or lack, and that makes people feel safe, seen, and inspired.

Her Influence is subtle but unmistakable. Zimmy doesn't try to convince or persuade. She simply shows up as she is: congruent, kind, and anchored. That presence alone moves people. Her way of being invites others into greater alignment with themselves. She speaks the truth gently, listens without judgment, and sets boundaries with warmth and clarity. Emotional safety feels natural around her, not performative but a lived reality.

Then there's Excellence, not perfection, in her way of living with alignment, direction, and courage. Zimmy's life reflects the essence of dynamic responsiveness. She doesn't need to control every outcome, because she trusts herself to meet life moment to moment. She brings her whole self to what she's doing, fully engaged and fully alive, and her wholehearted presence and timely action are the signatures of her Excellence. She doesn't try to be extraordinary, but she shows up anchored in self-worth, clear and consistent on her path, living courageously and with purpose.

Zimmy's journey shows how the Way of the Catalyst emerges as an intuitive way of living when the heart is pure and the head is clear. Her ability to turn inward, quiet the noise, take one step at a time, and extend genuine kindness without exaggeration or pretense has led her to a rich and fulfilling life shaped by sharing and receiving from a place of abundance. Abundance is not about having more; it's about knowing you are enough, trusting there is enough, and engaging with the world with that inner sense of wholeness. Zimmy lives from that space every day, in every aspect of her life, with grace and ease.

While Zimmy's path unfolded through personal healing and purpose-driven work with children and communities, the next story takes us into a different setting—the world of business, leadership, and organizational change. This is where we meet Michel, whose journey shows how one person with a clear big picture and catalytic attitudes can drive change that is both strategically sound and deeply human.

9
Michel: The Catalyst Leader

I met Michel during the leadership retreat I mentioned in Chapter One. He had just returned to the Netherlands after five years working as an expat in Africa for a Dutch multinational, one of the Fortune Global 500 companies.

Upon his return, Michel joined the executive board of a Dutch operating company just before they decided to sell their logistics and wholesale operations arm to a specialized partner, aiming to enhance distribution services and operational efficiency.

Michel supported the idea from a strategic point of view and was appointed to lead the divestment of the entire business unit, an assignment that would affect over 600 employees across eleven sites. However, the task came with no plan, no buyer, and no defined process. The only thing that was clear was that it wouldn't be easy.

When Michel stepped into his role as director, he began the usual round of introductions. Still, in the back of his mind, he kept thinking, "Everybody I'm saying 'hello' to now, I will eventually have to say 'goodbye' to." At that stage, the people he was meeting had no knowledge of the executive committee's decision.

"Some of the employees who had to be transferred had been with the company for more than twenty or thirty years," Michel said. "It's a very iconic company. People were proud to work there and were deeply emotionally attached to the brand. But if they wanted to honor their employment contract, they had to move."

Michel was determined to lead the transition in a way that aligned with his values and principles. This wasn't just about hitting targets, ensuring development, or overseeing execution. He knew that the decision was inevitable, but he also knew that the one thing he could influence was how it was carried out.

Michel's challenge was to get the job done while honoring the mental and emotional impact it would have on everyone involved. He knew the process had to be more than practical; it had to be deeply human.

He designed an approach that incorporated both. Anticipating the emotional toll, Michel took the time to understand the stages of grief, which he expected many of the people affected by the decision would experience.

Michel's eight-step process for leading change

In parallel with the negotiation process with the potential buyers, Michel spent six to eight months preparing for the shift before the announcement was made. During that time, he created an eight-step process to guide the transition—a roadmap that balanced business strategy with care for the people impacted. It was his way of staying anchored in integrity while leading them through the disruptive change. What follows is Michel's eight-step process, in his own words.

Step One: A story that makes sense

"The main concern was: How do I deal with this in a healthy, respectful way, and still get it done?

"A lot of pre-work had to be done. Before announcing a change of this scale, the story needs to be in order. Part of that story must explain the strategic rationale behind the decision, and at the same time, it must address people's mental and emotional needs. I allowed myself time to find a way to tell the story that was honest, clear, and in language that people could truly understand, without corporate jargon. I wasn't under the illusion that it would be accepted immediately, but I wanted it to be accessible, grounded in truth, and tailored to each group.

"When I found the right buyer, a Dutch family-owned business, I started to get a sense of how they operated and the kind of people they were. Those insights helped me shape the narrative I would use to announce the change lying ahead. This part was critical. Everything that followed, all the next steps, would rest on the success of that first announcement. The message had to be clear and credible, even though the content was difficult.

"The first version of the story was for the 600 employees who were being transferred to the new company. That narrative was the most complex because it had to carry both the business reasoning and the human weight of what this meant for them. Nevertheless, I avoided complicated mergers and acquisitions language. The second version of the story was for the shareholders, focused more on the strategic side of the decision."

Step Two: Announcement day

"The second step was communicating the decision to the managers in my division, who would then help deliver the announcement across all eleven sites on the same day. We made sure everyone was present at those meetings. It was important that every individual felt equally respected, and that they heard the news directly from us, not secondhand. My managers and I rehearsed the announcement thoroughly, ensuring we were all aligned in delivering the same message at the same time.

"We formed announcement teams composed of our leadership team, representatives from the buyer, and members of our HR department to facilitate the Q&A sessions afterward. The process was carefully structured to reduce confusion and minimize the space for assumptions. We aimed to be as clear and respectful as possible with everyone receiving the message.

"Once such news is shared, you're not in control of how people process it or what happens in their minds. That's why preparing the story and setting up the moment of announcement with care is so crucial. People will remember how they received this kind of news. They might not like it, but they can still respect how it was communicated.

"There's an important question every leader should ask in such moments: 'Are you explaining the decision purely from the company's point of view, or are you helping people understand what it means for them?' The latter is what truly makes the difference. Once the message is shared, it needs to be repeated whenever necessary until it sinks in. The repetition must be delivered with patience and consistency."

Step Three: Seek and use feedback

"The third step was staying attuned to people's feedback and being present and connected, not just in formal meeting rooms, but in informal settings like coffee breaks, hallway conversations, and near the water cooler. My managers and I made a conscious effort to gather information about how the news had landed for people across the sites. Moreover, we didn't just collect feedback; we acted on it. Sometimes that meant addressing concerns directly, adjusting our pace, or offering more clarity on what people could expect.

"We made it a point not to sugarcoat the message or beat around the bush. It has to be clear. You can't tell people, 'We're doing this, but nothing's going to change for you.' That would be like announcing the biggest news and immediately denying its impact, which simply isn't true. Even though many things would stay the same, such as their job roles and compensation, the reality was that they were moving to a different company. That matters. The focus needed to be not on what would stay the same, but on what would change and how we would go about managing that change. It's important to expect that, once the news is out, you're less in control, and you must deal with what comes.

"We informed a few key people about what was coming, clarified their role in the process, and asked for their support in helping their teams during the transition. I was aware that people weren't exactly eager to talk to me. I was, after all, the one who had come in, and, six months later, the business was sold. At times, it felt like the messenger was resented more than the message itself.

"I was aware of what I could and couldn't do. My role was to deliver a clear message and to remain consistent, mindful, and respectful throughout. I made myself as visible, approachable, and available as possible for people to share how the news had landed and what mattered most to them.

"Of course, I couldn't do that alone. I relied on other managers and key team members to support the process. I turned to colleagues with whom I had a direct relationship, since there was already a level of trust established between us. I asked them for help in being present in the field, connecting with people, getting a sense of how they felt about the news, and highlighting what concerns we needed to address, bearing in mind the inevitability of the transfer.

"We used this feedback to inform the second wave of announcements. In some cases, we brought in representatives from the buyer to speak directly with the teams. Acting on real feedback instead of relying on assumptions helped us pace the process in a way that stayed connected to the people. It was essential that, at the very least, the majority of people accepted the transition. Support would be ideal, but acceptance was the minimum needed for progress to take root."

Step Four: Go slow to go fast

"Some companies push the process through, and it works in the sense that the deal gets done. Then, six to twelve months later, people leave or become disengaged, and the buyer is left with a messy situation. That would have impacted us directly because, after the transition, the buyer was going to supply our logistics operations in the future. If things didn't land well, it would come back to us, not just ethically, but also operationally.

"It was critical to give people the space and time they needed for the initial shock to settle before integrating them into the new company. We knew that most would go through the five stages of grief, as described by the psychiatrist Elisabeth Kübler-Ross: denial, anger, bargaining, sadness, and finally acceptance.[23] We paid close attention to where people were in the cycle and responded accordingly. I noticed that once people had the chance to express their anger, they moved more quickly toward acceptance.

"The impact of such news creates a fork in the road. Some people leave, while others accept it and stay. In our case, the majority stayed. Why? Because they saw that we weren't playing games. We didn't try to sugarcoat the situation or minimize its significance. Despite their initial shock, they recognized that we were handling this in a healthy, respectful way. We were present. We were available. We listened to their concerns and kept moving forward with the project."

Step Five: Integrate the first accepters

"The first group of 'accepters' began to emerge once the project leadership team had demonstrated consistency in both message and support. These were the people who started to see the positive potential in the change. It became essential to enroll them in facilitating the transition.

"You can recognize the early accepters of change in subtle ways, sometimes in what they say casually over coffee, and other times in the steady, constructive way they comport themselves at work. Once we identified them, we paired them with team members from the buyer's company. We gave them the broader context, the strategic direction, and the space to figure out the details together, as they knew better than we did how to interlink the day-to-day workflow.

"When people from both companies began working side by side, something powerful happened: the sense of 'us' versus 'them' began to dissolve. Our early accepters started to see that the buyers were just like us—people who wanted to do good work, avoid unnecessary stress, contribute to a healthy work environment, and be fairly compensated.

"This shift sparked a ripple effect. More people began accepting the change and wanted to be part of those early integration stages. Eventually, we hit a pivot point, where almost everyone began to move. That momentum wouldn't have been possible without first identifying and engaging the initial group of accepters. We clarified the strategic outcome with them, gave them responsibility for working out the details in a way they knew best, and trusted them to lead that phase. There was some flexibility in how the result would take shape, but we were aligned on where it needed to land."

Step Six: Set them up for success

"Our people entered the new company's environment well-prepared. They understood the cultural differences they were stepping into, moving from a multinational setting to a family-owned business with an entirely different way of working. We invested significant effort in setting them up for success, not for conflict. Of course, some tension did arise because we couldn't control everything, but we made sure it remained manageable.

"When conflict did surface, we intervened promptly. We didn't let it drag on for more than a few days. Our approach was to normalize conflict, bring both parties back into dialogue, help them refocus on the task at hand, and reconnect them with the bigger picture. We did this consistently, over and over again, until the two merging teams began to work together in harmony.

"During intervention meetings, I would often use a simple but powerful exercise. I placed two chairs directly facing each other, which is a negotiation stance. It quickly became like a ping-pong match, with one side saying, 'But we've done it this way for fifteen years, and it works well,' and the other making the same point in different words. Frustration would only grow. This happens often in mergers and acquisitions where, even after the deal is signed, the 'chairs' stay facing each other, locked in opposition. You can't blame people for hitting a dead end when the setup itself makes collaboration difficult.

"So, I would turn both chairs 45° to be side by side and introduce a third chair facing them. Now, instead of staring each other down, both people were facing the same direction. Then, I'd say:

> 'Now your job is to come up with the best way to make this new combination work. It might not be your way or your way; it could be a third option you create together. You have the functional expertise; we're not here to dictate how to do it. We trust that you've got this.
>
> 'The negotiation phase is over. The more each side defends its own way, the more

stuck we all become. Now we're in the stage of integration, bringing teams, operations, and knowledge together, and we need your flexibility to create one coherent plan that works for the whole company. We have seven functional areas to align. Let's build something that fits them all.'"

Step Seven: Give it time

"This 'turning the chairs' approach, helping people shift from opposition to co-creation, was something we introduced early on. But it takes time for people to go from 10% collaboration to 70% or 80%, and that's normal. Eventually, though, it works. After a while, people continue the process on their own, sitting side by side, facing the same direction, sorting out their issues together.

"You simply can't rush the beginning. If you do, you risk people either leaving altogether or staying without truly engaging, doing the bare minimum just to get by. In our case, that risk was off the table for two reasons. First, because of the people. I believe a work environment should be healthy and empowering. Second, because of the business. We were signing a fifteen-year contract with the new company to provide our operational services. If we had mishandled the transition, we would have shot ourselves in the foot for the next decade and a half.

"There are a few key elements that help bring out the best in people during a transition like this:

- Being honest about the message, so people know what to expect.
- Normalizing the difficulty of the situation so that people don't feel alone in their experience.
- Empowering people as early as possible with a systems-level perspective, like the one we used in the chairs exercise, so they can clearly see the bigger picture and their role within it.

"We gave people the tools to move forward. The content and day-to-day operational details were theirs to co-create and synchronize. Eventually, you reach a point where each team has done its part of the integration. And then, you bring it all together and let the ship sail."

Step Eight: Communicate with consistency

"The full integration process took about twelve to eighteen months. Whenever we noticed people slipping back into the negotiating mindset, we brought them back to the reality: negotiation is over, we're now in integration. Each time a new group joined the process, we repeated the same practice. We'd bring them into a room and open a dialogue about what mattered, how they planned to collaborate, and how they would move the merger forward together.

"Communication had to be ongoing and intentional. We weren't just working with the sixty to seventy people actively involved in shaping the merger; we also had 500 others doing their day-to-day jobs. They weren't directly involved in integration meetings, but they were still deeply part of the transition. We made the effort to keep them informed, to give them the opportunity to respond to what was happening, and to stay connected to the process.

"In these types of transitions, communication is often underestimated. Here's the truth: if you inform only once, you haven't informed at all. You have to re-inform. Reiterate. Follow up. Again and again. This kind of work requires patience; it's not a crash project you can complete in two or three months and walk away from. It takes time, consistency, and presence.

"This isn't a linear process. People leave, others join, and you have to get each started in the right way. That's why we developed a strong communication strategy from the beginning, to ensure that information was shared clearly, consistently, and in a way that reached everyone involved.

"Think of it like this: you start by communicating a message to four people. That grows to forty, then to 400. The most intensive work happens in that shift from four to forty, because if your message is honest and clear, it will carry itself from there. It will spread naturally, in hallways, during coffee breaks, and in everyday conversations.

"However, if what spreads is an interpretation of your message, and not the real thing, you're guaranteed chaos. That kind of confusion is hard to contain and even harder to repair. Clarity and honesty in communication don't just build trust; they save time, energy, and unnecessary fallout."

Inner anchors: What held Michel steady

When I asked Michel what helped him stay centered through such a complex and emotionally charged process, he shared that his main concern was to "do it right."

He was delivering a message that rarely inspires gratitude toward the messenger. Fortunately, the lead time he had before the formal announcement gave him space to process the change internally before guiding others through it. The one benchmark he held onto was simple: "Can I look at myself in the mirror and say I did this in a way that aligns with my principles?"

This forward-looking question shaped how he approached communication—being transparent about what was going to happen, listening openly to feedback, and acting on it where possible, all while being honest about the non-negotiables. The decision had already been made; what mattered to Michel was carrying it out with integrity.

He made peace early on with the fact that not everyone would appreciate his efforts—definitely not at first, and maybe not even in the end. While he had worked in the Netherlands before, it was past experience in one of Africa's most challenging countries that shaped his resilience and sharpened his ability to navigate conflict, uncertainty, and crisis. It had made him ready to lead this transition.

Michel's method was simple, yet effective: stay calm, get the right information before making decisions, and respond in small, thoughtful steps to see how they land. He said, "When there's resistance, tension, or uncertainty, that structure matters. I've seen leaders react quickly, rush to fix everything at once, and it often goes wrong. Small moves allow space for realignment."

He chose to position himself at the center of the tension to be present in conflicts, confrontations, and disagreements. Even when people didn't want to talk or were preparing to protest, he stayed. Unless they walked him out of the room, he stayed and listened. That consistency built trust and softened resistance over time.

To Michel, setbacks weren't failures; they were moments for realignment. He didn't let difficulty defeat him. He learned, adapted, and moved forward. He said, "If you can get it to work eight out of ten times, that's success. The rest is about repair and restart, as quickly as possible. One of the biggest lessons I've learned is that when you mess up, you can still make it right, most of the time. Maybe not immediately, but if you've been consistent, people will give you space to course-correct.

"That's what I've come to understand: consistency isn't perfection. It's showing up in alignment with your values most of the time and owning it when you fall short. That builds trust. And humor helps too, especially when it's self-directed. It's part of who I am. It lightens the tension and makes the process more human."

Michel led the transition with the long view in mind. He took the time upfront to scope properly, listen deeply, and connect teams. He didn't rush the process to meet a timeline. He understood that people would remember how they were treated. People may not have chosen the change, but a catalytic leader helped them feel seen, respected, and taken seriously throughout. That's where real engagement happens.

"If you do it right," he said, "even if it takes longer, it can last for fifteen years. But if you push it through in three months, it can fall apart within one."

Michel's steadiness came from a clear internal compass. He anchored himself in his guiding principles, leveraged his experience, stayed calm under pressure, responded in small, deliberate steps, welcomed feedback, and sustained progress without rush or any meaningless compromises. That's what held him steady, and that's what helped others around him steady themselves too.

Michel's leadership: A catalytic lens

Michel's story is a powerful example of catalytic leadership in action. Much like a chemical catalyst, he enabled transformation with minimal stress—reducing resistance, creating momentum, and shaping outcomes without being consumed in the process.

What follows is an exploration of how Michel embodied the Five Attitudes of the Catalyst: Responsibility, Proactivity, Interdependence, Influence, and Excellence. Each is brought to life through his decisions, presence, and interactions.

While each of the Five Attitudes stands on its own, they are also interlinked, working together to bring catalysis into everyday life. Certain pairs naturally complete and reinforce each other. Responsibility and Influence, for instance, are two sides of the same coin. What begins internally as ownership of one's emotions, thoughts, and stories (Responsibility) becomes a stabilizing presence that creates a meaningful impact without force (Influence).

Similarly, Proactivity and Excellence are extensions of each other. Proactivity acts as the inner compass, through living life by design and taking conscious action, while Excellence is its outward expression, revealed in how we engage with the world around us, moment to moment, with alignment, clarity, and courage. These pairs move from the inside out, forming a bridge between inner mastery and the ripple effect of our actions, often extending beyond our immediate awareness.

Interdependence, then, becomes the turning point. It's where the inner world opens and meets the external environment. This is where "me" turns into "we" and generates a collective momentum that elevates everyone involved *because* of their differences, not despite them.

Responsibility and Influence

Michel accepted early on that his role wouldn't always be met with appreciation, and yet he took on the assignment for two reasons: first, because it made sense from a strategic perspective, and second, because he knew he could lead the process with integrity, while staying mindful of the impact that the change would have on people. His inner narrative about why he was doing it was clear and in harmony with his principles. His clarity, emotional awareness, and steady presence reflected the essence of Responsibility: choosing how to respond, and doing so in a way that reinforced trust, alignment, and clarity.

He dedicated six to eight months to preparing the ground before a single announcement was made. That time wasn't just about logistics; it was about finding the right buyer and crafting a narrative that was honest, clear, and made sense to the people involved. Throughout the process, he remained present and consistent. He communicated openly, patiently, and at a pace people could absorb. Even in tense moments, he stayed steady and accessible. His calm and honest approach created an environment where people felt safe enough to process, respond, and gradually begin to collaborate. Without pushing or rushing, Michel encouraged movement through presence, attunement, and clear communication that met people where they were.

Proactivity and Excellence

Michel didn't simply react to a directive from the executive committee. He designed an eight-step process to lead a high-stakes, emotionally charged transition with foresight and intention. He took conscious ownership of how the change would unfold, rehearsing announcements with his managers, preparing people for each stage of integration, and equipping them with tools to stay engaged and empowered. He kept moving forward through moments of conflict, confrontation, and uncertainty, even when the emotional weight was heavy. His ability to stay intentional and resilient in the face of challenge reflects a deeply proactive mindset that creates possibility, takes deliberate action, and persists under pressure.

Rather than taking a passive or detached stance, Michel chose to stay engaged, present, and responsive, moment to moment. His self-worth wasn't tied to being liked or validated, but to staying honest, clear, and consistent. His commitment to being able to look himself in the mirror once the project was complete became his compass. Alignment with his principles anchored him throughout the process, much like the Big Picture Personal Canvas does for the Catalyst. Whether he was confronting conflict, listening to resistance, seeking feedback, or simply holding space in silence, Michel didn't step aside or hand the hard parts over to others. He met each moment with presence and intention, making direction, courage, and adaptability the foundations of his leadership.

Interdependence

At every step, Michel intentionally involved others, from his managers to early accepters, to HR and the buyer's representatives, trusting them to co-create and lead parts of the process. He empowered employees to shape an integrated workflow in ways that made sense on the ground, confident in their capacity to find practical solutions. He was clear and direct about the challenges ahead, refusing to sugarcoat or avoid the difficult conversations. Normalizing conflict, being transparent about what was unfolding, and asking for help when needed was a vulnerable stance, yet it earned trust and respect. The "chairs exercise" reflected how he moved people out of opposition and into an interdependent space in which to build something new.

After completing this restructuring project, Michel left the corporate world and went on to offer his services as an independent business consultant specializing in mergers and acquisitions. What he carries forward is more than expertise; it's a lived embodiment of catalytic leadership. Through Responsibility, he anchored himself in principled living. With Proactivity, he designed the path forward with intention. He practiced Interdependence by sharing power and placing trust in others and in himself. His Influence came through presence, clarity, and consistency, not force. In each moment, he brought Excellence by meeting complexity with inner alignment, clarity, and courage.

Michel didn't just lead a transition; he became the catalyst for an all-around successful project. By staying grounded in the attitudes of the Catalyst, he helped transform not only an organization but also the way people experienced a disruptive change.

That's the essence of catalysis: making transformation possible with minimal pressure, without being diminished or consumed in the process.

10
Becoming The Catalyst

Reshaping your attitudes may be one of the most difficult yet most rewarding changes you'll ever make. It's difficult because it requires inner work: bringing unconscious patterns into conscious awareness and deliberately shifting toward a healthier, more effective set of thoughts, feelings, and behaviors. It's rewarding because life begins to respond to you in ways that reflect your refined inner stance.

We'll begin by exploring where individuals and organizations often get stuck. From there, we'll move into the shift itself—tuning in to both internal and external feedback, using the Big Picture Personal Canvas as a tool for alignment, and intentionally embodying the Five Attitudes of the Catalyst. The aim is to create sustainable change with less pressure and greater ease for yourself and those around you.

"This is me" syndrome

When life calls for change, many people experience inner resistance that can manifest in making excuses for maintaining the status quo, arguing in defense of their limitations, or retreating into familiar patterns.

A "this is me" mindset confuses rigidity with authenticity and hides behind the language of self-acceptance. It reflects an inner resistance to change, and it is used to deflect feedback about a personal trait or habit. For example, someone might pride themselves on being direct, but that same "directness" might sometimes be viewed as intimidating or even shaming by others, resulting in their advice falling flat.

The reason is simple: that approach defeats its own purpose. If the goal is to raise awareness, inspire change, or create forward momentum, shaming shuts that door. It triggers the fight-or-flight response, blocks creative thinking, and disconnects people from your message.

They might believe others should accept their attitude, because after all, "that's just who I am," and their intentions are good. But good intentions alone don't get the job done. When we take a closer look at what "this is me" really means, we might discover that it's not our true, capable, adult self speaking, but rather a set of redundant habits formed early in life. These patterns may have once helped us feel safe, accepted, or successful, but over time, they stop serving us in new contexts. Left unexamined, they harden into default strategies that limit our growth. The sooner we stop defending them, the richer and more meaningful our lives become.

The same principle applies to communities and organizations. On a collective level, "this is me" becomes "this is us" or "That's how we've always done things." These cultural norms are shaped by founders or early authority figures, whose values became the foundation of the group's identity. Over time, those norms sink into the group's subconscious and often go unquestioned, simply because they've always been there.

When the glass slipper no longer fits

"This is us" in an organizational culture context reflects what I refer to as the glass slipper mentality, a once-perfect fit that eventually becomes a constraint. No one dares to question it because of the story behind it.

In a fast-growing design agency, the origin story was sacred. Years ago, the founder, a brilliant and meticulous creative, built the company from scratch with a small team of like-minded perfectionists. They prided themselves on going "above and beyond," staying late, obsessing over details, and never compromising on aesthetics. Clients raved, awards followed, and slowly, the hustle-and-polish culture hardened into its identity.

A decade later, the agency has grown ten times in size. Teams are cross-functional. Deadlines are tighter. Burnout is real. New hires bring in fresh ideas about agile processes, inclusive creativity, and sustainable pace, but whenever someone suggests doing things differently, the old guard bristles: "That's not how we do things here. This might work elsewhere, but it's not how we earned our name. Our clients expect nothing less than perfection."

What started as a shared value of creative excellence has slipped into a rigid performance script. People are no longer asking, "What's the most effective way to meet the needs of the moment?" Instead, they are squeezing themselves into a legacy culture that no longer fits. It needs an upgrade that accounts for the business's expansion and the diverse needs of its people.

This is the glass slipper mentality in action. A beautiful story, a perfect fit… once. Now, it's cutting off their circulation. Yet, no one dares to break it. Because the slipper isn't just a method; it's a myth. It says: "To be here, you must contort to this shape or go barefoot."

The reality is that what worked in the past may no longer serve the needs of the present or the future.

Without reflection and renewal, group identity can become as rigid as individual identity, resisting the very change it needs to evolve and thrive.

Personal transformation: An inside-out journey

The immediate world around us is a generous source of feedback for inner growth and transformation. Often, the unpleasant experiences deliver the most powerful pointers, because they command our attention and nudge us forward. Internal feedback shows up as a sense of dissatisfaction or nonacceptance in a certain area of your life. Both internal and external feedback can become our greatest motivation to grow and evolve.

The instinctive response, however, typically involves outward solutions—leaving a job, ending a relationship, or moving to a new place. While these external steps may indeed be valid and sometimes necessary, they rarely address the core issue. Without an internal shift, the same patterns of thought and behavior tend to recreate similar outcomes. A popular metaphor in personal development illustrates this beautifully. Imagine trying to clean a blemish you see while looking in the mirror by wiping the mirror itself. That's what change looks like when we only pursue it on the outside.

Taking external action can feel satisfying, and it often offers relief, because you get a sense that you are doing something about it. But that relief is usually temporary. The deeper questions are:

- "Is this the right action?"
- "What am I trying to accomplish by taking this action?"
- "Where do I need more clarity? What within me needs to shift?"

Taking time to reflect on this early on can save us significant time, energy, and effort. The clarity we gain allows us to take focused, intentional action aligned with our big picture, which leads to more meaningful results.

Tune in to what's calling your attention and begin with one step. For example, feeling unfulfilled in your work might be more than a sign of a poor fit. It could be a deeper invitation to realign your sense of meaning and purpose. It may be time to work on your self-awareness, clarify what matters to you today, build new skills, or shift direction in a way that honors your Big Picture Personal Canvas.

In the same way, if you're struggling in a relationship and can't accept someone's dysfunctional behavior, it may be pointing you inward, toward your role in the dynamic. Ask yourself:

- Am I neglecting my responsibility to speak up or honor my boundaries?
- Am I tolerating too much out of fear, habit, or lack of hope?
- Am I unintentionally creating an emotional environment that feels unsafe for us to connect?

Reflecting honestly on your internal process can clarify what's truly fueling the struggle and what needs to shift.

Whatever your specific challenge, this is your entry point to personal transformation. Begin with one small, honest change and stay with it long enough for it to become natural. Over time, small, consistent, internal shifts lead to meaningful external changes that are sustainable. Transformation doesn't start with the mirror; it starts with the person looking into it.

Living the Way of the Catalyst

You've been introduced to the Way of the Catalyst—my developmental model for personal and relational mastery. It offers a structured yet flexible approach to deepening self-awareness, intentionally activating effective attitudes, and creating meaningful impact in the social spaces in which we live and work.

The journey began with your Big Picture Personal Canvas—a framework to help you clarify your direction, principles, and desired outcomes across the Physical, Emotional, Mental, and Social (PEMS) dimensions of life.

From there, the journey progressed through the Five Attitudes of the Catalyst. Each attitude offered a set of three traits that can support your growth and help you engage more effectively with the world around you.

This is not a fixed formula, but a living framework. What follows are starting points—thought triggers, practices, and tools you can explore in your own way. Some may resonate deeply. Others may not be relevant right now. Take what fits, open up to new meaning, and return to any part as you evolve.

The Way of the Catalyst is designed to grow with you, not to define you. You are the one who brings this model to life through your reflections, choices, and commitment to living as a Catalyst—someone who creates meaningful impact, with more grace and less struggle, without being consumed in the process.

Let this be your new beginning where you define your Big Picture Personal Canvas and intentionally bring the Five Attitudes of the Catalyst to life.

Your Big Picture Personal Canvas

The journey begins with clarity. Your Big Picture Personal Canvas is the foundation for the Way of the Catalyst. It invites you to step back from the noise of daily demands and reconnect with what truly matters to you.

Once internalized and integrated, your big picture becomes your compass, offering guidance, strength, and reassurance. It reflects your personal design across the PEMS dimensions—Physical, Emotional, Mental, and Social. When these dimensions are aligned, you move with more intention and ease. When they're out of sync, you may experience more confusion, reactivity, and disconnection—signals inviting you to pause and realign.

This canvas is not about crafting a perfect life vision. It's a living, evolving tool for you to revisit, refine, and realign over time. You can use it to guide your overall life direction or to gain clarity about a specific situation, relationship, or transition.

Whenever you feel stuck or scattered, return to these three anchoring questions:

1. Why am I here? (What is my role or purpose in this space, relationship, or situation?)
2. Where is this pointing me? (What is this experience bringing to my attention?)

3. What do I truly want? (Beneath the surface, what am I really seeking?)

Let these questions become part of your inner dialogue. Use them to shape your days with greater clarity and filter your decisions so that they align with a big picture that is meaningful to you.

When you live with big picture clarity, you stop chasing what doesn't matter and start creating from a place of focus and confidence.

Attitude One: Responsibility

You can only go as far as your inner narrative allows you. Most limitations don't come from circumstances; they come from interpretations. Change the story, and you shift the experience. Reframing your inner narrative to reflect where you're going, not just where you've been or where you are now, creates subtle but powerful shifts in your thoughts and emotions. The old story got you here, and it may have served you well, but a new chapter often requires a new narrative.

R1: Awareness of emotional states and their impact

The first step is to become emotionally aware. Start by checking in with how you feel, without judgment.

Name the emotion (using Gloria Willcox's Feeling Wheel can help you name it specifically).[24] Then look inward and ask:

- What story am I telling myself that's fueling this feeling?
- How is this emotion shaping my attitudes, behaviors, or choices right now?

For example, if you feel resentment:

- What story is playing in my head?
- What assumptions or interpretations are influencing the way I'm showing up?

This level of observation gives you the ability to pause, reflect, and recognize the assumptions and interpretations that are driving how you think, feel, and act. Refer back to Chapter Two (The Big Picture Personal Canvas), "The Emotional," for tools to support this step.

R2: Mastery in selecting emotions for effectiveness

This step is about emotional agility—your ability to consciously shift your emotional state to serve a deliberate outcome. Once you've named and processed an emotion, you can begin to consciously select a more empowering one and reframe the story in your head to match the desired emotion.

You're hardly ever stuck with the emotion itself, only with the story behind it. Ask yourself:

- What emotion would serve me better right now?
- What story would support that emotion and move me forward?

Then practice telling a new story that is also true and relevant.

For example, if you're feeling despair, you may be stuck in the details of a challenging moment. Zoom out to reconnect with the bigger picture. You may find yourself accessing emotions like acceptance, surrender, or even hope.

This is not about denying or bypassing your emotions. It's about recognizing that there is more than what you're feeling in the moment—a bigger picture that matters, too. When you connect to that, your focus naturally expands and the emotional intensity begins to soften, allowing you to rewrite the narrative to one that supports your big picture and who you are becoming.

R3: Making a life-affirming choice every time

Every moment presents a choice, and every choice shapes your life. This step is about making small, enlivening choices that align with your Big Picture Personal Canvas.

If your big picture were a painting, would the small, pixel-like choices you're making each day add up to create the vision you truly want? A series of small, intentional choices in the right direction leads to meaningful, lasting results. For example, pause before replying to a message that triggers you, saying "yes" to yet another commitment, judging yourself or someone else, or rushing to protect yourself from a perceived threat. Take a couple of deep breaths. Reconnect with your principles and your big picture. Then choose a response that honors who you are becoming, not who you've been or even who you are right now when under pressure.

When you practice these three traits—awareness, emotional agility, and life-affirming choice—you shift from reacting to life to actively shaping it.

Attitude Two: Proactivity

Remember: life is like a lump of clay; what you create with it is up to you. Proactivity engages your mental faculties to interpret your current reality objectively, imagine a desired outcome that aligns with your Big Picture Personal Canvas, and map out a process to get there. The process isn't necessarily clear all at once. It often unfolds with progress. This is where your Integrated Time Awareness comes into play (see Chapter One: Change).

Draw on lessons from the past, envision a future that is mindful of the present but not bound by it, and begin living elements of that future now by leveraging your inner and outer resources. The more intentionally you bring aspects of your envisioned future into the present, the more powerfully you move ahead—not by waiting for change, but by becoming it, here and now.

P1: Recognizing one's own role in creating possibilities

Proactivity begins with setting your priorities in order. Identify where your time and energy are being drained and repurpose that toward what matters most before any issues escalate.

Initiate the attitudes and behaviors you want others to embody and remain consistent in demonstrating them. Be conscious of your role in perpetuating unwanted situations. For example, imagine feeling frustrated with a person who matters to you because they go off on tangents and get easily sidetracked in conversations. Clarity is important to you, and you want them to communicate with focus and precision.

You come to realize that your frustration is only making things worse. You reframe the story in your head from "Their way of communicating confuses me," to "It is challenging for them to clearly express their thoughts." This helps clarify your understanding of them and enables you to support them to express their thoughts by asking questions, confirming your understanding, summarizing the conversation, and checking in with them to ensure you understood them correctly.

Staying consistent in demonstrating clarity, asking them for what you need moving forward—a clear, precise articulation of your thoughts—and offering to help when necessary, is the approach that's most likely to influence a shift in that person's level of communication. Your input alone changes the outcome and creates a new possibility that shifts your environment in meaningful ways.

P2: Taking action by conscious choice

Random actions produce random results. Start with one area of your life, relationship, or situation that leaves you deeply dissatisfied. Now imagine you have to live with it for the next ten years. What would that be like?

Take time to reflect and prepare for a shift. In the heat of the moment, especially when you're first building this practice, focused and deliberate action is harder. Start by visualizing the triggering moment and your immediate reaction to it. Notice the inner narrative that arises. Then, gently shake it off, and re-visualize the same situation, this time seeing yourself respond in a way that aligns with your big picture and who you are becoming. Notice the difference. It might feel easier to go with the automatic response, because it's a habit. But it's far more powerful in the long run to pause, think, and take intentional action in the direction of your big picture.

Repeating this process of visualizing alternative responses and integrating new patterns leads to making proactivity second nature.

P3: Demonstrating inner resilience

Every time you make a decision, you live with the consequences. Every time you take a new path, your environment will challenge you to revert to old ways. Human systems often gravitate back to familiar patterns, seeking comfort in the known over uncertainty and transformation. Expect resistance; even positive change is often met with discomfort.

Be clear on your "why" and secure the PEMS aspects of your Big Picture Personal Canvas. Learn practical tools to stay grounded—physically, emotionally, and mentally—under pressure. Eliminate, or at least limit, contact with those who drain your energy. Instead, surround yourself with a few people who add value and meaning to your experience.

Manage your expectations and remain unattached to specific outcomes. Relying heavily on things unfolding in a particular way can become a slippery slope toward despair. Remember, you can't control everything, but you can manage yourself and navigate whatever life brings your way. Proactivity isn't about forcing outcomes. It's about taking an active role in shaping them with presence and agency.

Attitude Three: Interdependence

Discover what makes you uniquely you and how you naturally stand out from the crowd. Build your awareness of yourself and those around you. Learn to become the best version of yourself—with appreciation and compassion for both your strengths and limitations, and for the unique journeys of those around you.

There is no single path to Interdependence. What matters is your willingness to explore what enhances your self-awareness, builds character, and leads to self-mastery, so that you can contribute meaningfully within your social space.

As you progress through this process, you naturally deepen your understanding of others—their strengths, their limitations, and their differences. This is the foundation of an interdependent environment, where people don't compete to dominate but, instead, share power and co-create.

I1: Confidence in oneself

Lasting confidence doesn't come from appearance, status, or validation. It comes from your ability to learn, evolve, and navigate life in alignment with your Big Picture Personal Canvas.

Your ability to grow is a solid source of confidence that holds steady as circumstances change because it's grounded in resourcefulness and creativity. Your greatest power doesn't come from what you do or what you have, but from who you are. Do not settle for "this is me" if it means staying stuck in confusion, disconnection, or ineffectiveness. That version of you may have once been a survival strategy, but it's not your destiny. Unconfuse yourself. Find meaning. Learn how to be the best version of yourself.

Here are a few modalities and frameworks that can support self-awareness, personal mastery, leadership development, effective communication, conflict resolution, and culture building:

- CliftonStrengths assessment, developed by Gallup: A tool designed to help individuals discover their unique patterns of thinking, feeling, and behaving, and categorize them into thirty-four CliftonStrengths' themes.[25]
- The Enneagram: A framework that maps nine core personality types, each revealing distinct motivations, fears, and growth paths.[26]
- TIFF profile: A functional fluency profile based on Transactional Analysis. It provides a personal behavioral profile showing how you

function in different contexts to help you become more self-aware, emotionally intelligent, and interpersonally effective.[27]

- The Egogram: A tool based on Transactional Analysis, it maps the intensity of five ego states and reveals behavioral tendencies and internal dynamics, offering a growth pathway.[28]
- DiSC: A tool that categorizes individuals into four primary personality styles to help them understand themselves and how to adapt to others.[29]
- Insights Discovery: A tool based on the psychology of Carl Jung, using four color energies to represent different behavioral styles and ways to adapt to others.[30]

You don't need to master them all. Exploring one that resonates with you is enough, unless your curiosity leads you to discover more.

12: Comfort with vulnerability

Vulnerability often triggers discomfort. Our instinct is to relieve it quickly by hiding, defending, deflecting, masking, or pretending. Vulnerability can be real or imagined. In both cases, it impacts thoughts, feelings, and behavior. You might avoid asking for help, sugarcoat your real feelings, hold back your thoughts, or dismiss others' vulnerability with advice or humor.

Those strategies often backfire, and you ultimately find yourself more vulnerable than before.

It's important to acknowledge your own vulnerability and welcome the vulnerability of others. Fighting against it or avoiding it drives you away from deeply connecting in meaningful ways. Acknowledging your own vulnerability is evident when you ask for help, express your needs, take the risk of being rejected, speak your mind, and share your true feelings with respect and compassion in service of deepening the connection and expanding collaboration.

Acknowledging others' vulnerability is evident when you hold space for them to express themselves, process their emotions, or navigate challenges. It involves being present with empathy and compassion, without trying to fix, control, or direct the situation. Sometimes, all it takes is silence and patience. Other times, it takes active support and encouragement. In all cases, trust their power, wholeness, and resourcefulness. It's important to see the whole person, not just their vulnerabilities. Like you, others have the capacity to think, change, and grow through both their inner strengths and outer resources.

In a group context, identify the Big Picture Collective Canvas and let it guide your team's interactions. Having clarity on the shared big picture creates the sense of safety and permission that everyone needs to show up fully.

The building blocks of the Big Picture Collective Canvas are:

- **Physical:** What is the shared space that brings us together? For what purpose?
- **Emotional:** What emotional tone do we intend to create in this space? How is it being nurtured?
- **Mental:** In what ways are we smarter together? How are differences celebrated and appreciated? How does our space challenge and support the growth of each person involved?
- **Social:** What impact do we have on each other and on the wider world? What influence does our environment have on us? What shared intention are we holding?

13: Accepting of differences

As you develop your strengths and embrace your vulnerabilities, you'll find it easier to acknowledge and accept those of others.

Replace judgment with curiosity about deeper meaning and greater possibilities:

- What's behind this person's behavior? (Ask questions to understand.)
- What might they value that I don't see yet?

- What strength or perspective might be hidden in what I perceive as a flaw?

When you shift from labelling to wondering, from assuming to inquiring, you begin to uncover possibilities instead of problems. Synergy, not sameness, is the essence of Interdependence, with each person bringing their unique thread to a shared tapestry.

Attitude Four: Influence

Your true power to influence people often lies in your way of being, from the inside out. Consistent integrity—alignment in thought, word, and action—creates real, lasting impact on the world around you. That's the subtle strength of Influence; others feel it before they consciously understand it.

Take ownership of your impact. Make it an ongoing practice to refine how your presence, intentions, and attitudes affect others. When there's congruence between what you intend and what others actually experience, you are living in integrity, and that creates a ripple effect in your orbit.

Derive guidance from the Big Picture Collective Canvas. Notice when you're slipping into passivity—inaction, over-adaptation, agitation, incapacitation, or violence.[31] Identify your role and examine how you can guide yourself and others into an OK position, create psychological safety, and communicate clearly in a way that others can truly hear and understand.

F1: Navigating disarray in oneself and others

The more attuned you are with emotional and social intelligence, the quicker you'll notice signs of misalignment, both in yourself and others. Disarray can appear as tension, passive resistance, miscommunication, avoidance, or overreaction. It often begins subtly, before escalating into an overt conflict or breakdown.

The key is to catch it early. A drifting team member, a half-hearted "yes," or your own growing frustration are all signals. If left unaddressed, they can snowball into dysfunction, missed opportunities, or even a breakdown. For example, imagine you sense someone in your team is withdrawing from discussions. Rather than assuming they're disengaged, you pause and check in: "I noticed you've been quiet lately. Is everything alright?" This simple question may surface a hidden need or concern that, if ignored, could derail the collaboration.

Equally important, if someone has already stepped in, there's no need to do more. Hold space quietly. Influence is not about being heard or seen; it's about being attuned. Overcompensating or exaggerating erodes trust over time.

Approach disarray with awareness and curiosity. This is how you restore alignment with the shared big picture, before any damage is done.

F2: Creating effective safe spaces

You are always sending messages—through your posture, tone of voice, facial expressions, choice of words, and even silence. People respond more strongly to nonverbal cues than to your spoken words. If your words say, "I'm open," but your body signals tension or disapproval, people will respond to the nonverbal message.

To communicate a message that is congruent with the big picture:

- Take a few moments to check in with yourself—your thoughts, feelings, and stories—and align the inner part.
- Reflect on what brings you and others together.
- Consider the long-term impact of your input.
- Express yourself with clarity, precision, respect, and compassion.

Give space for others to share, and truly listen to them. Tune in to what's behind their words—emotion, hesitation, intent, or aspiration. Get curious about the meaning they assign to their words and expressions.

Seek feedback and do something with it. Do not treat it as a checkbox exercise, ticking it off the list just to say that you collected feedback, without real engagement, reflection, or care. Let it refine how you relate to others.

Be mindful when giving feedback. Appreciative feedback is best offered publicly and directed toward a person's being, e.g., "You're an exceptional leader." Constructive feedback is best given in private and directed toward their deeds. Start by acknowledging at least one thing you appreciate about the person or the intention behind their choice, then follow up with what needs to change, e.g., "Your presentation was clear and well-structured. Next time, you could avoid reading from the slides and instead engage with the audience more." Or, "I appreciate your intention to be there for me during this time. Right now, I need some space to process things on my own. I'll reach out when I'm ready. Thank you for your love and care."

Creating a safe space doesn't mean softening the truth; it means delivering it respectfully in a way that opens the space for progress. When people feel safe, they show up fully. That's when real collaboration begins.

F3: Tailoring communication to the listener

Your message is only as powerful as how well the listener understands it. It's not about what you say; it's about what they hear, interpret, and take in. Effective communication requires empathy, adaptability, and awareness of the other person's lens. It also requires you to check in and confirm understanding, especially in high-stakes or emotionally charged conversations. These are the unguarded moments when your awareness is most needed, and most easily forgotten.

You can revisit the tools from "I1: Confidence in oneself" to deepen your understanding of personality and behavioral differences. Here are a few additional frameworks that will help you tailor communication to your listeners:

- The Social Styles model by David Merrill and Roger Reid categorizes people by four interaction styles—driver, expressive, amiable, and analytical—and teaches you how to flex your communication accordingly.[32]
- Nonviolent Communication (NVC) by Marshall Rosenberg focuses on listening without judgment, expressing needs without blame, and building mutual understanding.[33]
- The Black Swan Group's "Three Negotiator Types" by Chris Voss classifies negotiation types as assertive, analytical, or accommodator to help flex your approach—especially useful in high-stakes conversations.[34]
- The Five Love Languages by Gary Chapman helps you understand how different people feel valued and appreciated. Later, the concept was adapted to a professional setting (see below).[35]

- The Five Languages of Appreciation in the Workplace by Gary Chapman and Paul White is a framework that helps leaders and teams express appreciation in ways that truly resonate. It offers practical strategies to improve workplace environments.[36]

These tools offer a general understanding of different styles and orientations. What matters most, however, is tuning in to the unique person in front of you and staying genuinely curious about their frame of reference. Adjusting how you communicate doesn't mean changing your message; it means making sure it's heard and received as you intend it to be.

Attitude Five: Excellence

Excellence is the pinnacle of the Five Attitudes. It's about bringing your dynamic self, moment to moment, and responding to life experiences with inner alignment, clear direction, and courage to take timely action.

Being responsive means you avoid leaving loose ends or things hanging. You complete what you set out to do. When something unexpected pops up, you handle it intentionally—either by resolving it immediately, parking it for later (and following through), or bringing appropriate closure to it. Imagine having three compartments, Now, Later, and Never, and choosing deliberately what belongs in each. Excellence calls for this kind of attentiveness, not only to the task at hand, but to all that surrounds it. It means accounting for both the seen and the unseen parts. For example, balancing strategy with culture, weighing the present alongside the future, and honoring the needs and contributions of all people involved. It's a wider lens that holds complexity without losing clarity of the big picture and the guiding principles of your life.

X1: Self-worth anchored in responsiveness to change

You may face challenges or setbacks you didn't anticipate. They can shake the ground beneath you and even make you question your readiness, identity, or capacity. In those moments, take the time to remember that you've been through change before, you've overcome situations that once felt challenging or even impossible, and in doing so, you became a new version of yourself.

When your sense of self-worth is anchored in responsiveness, it is no longer dependent on getting something right, having certainty, or maintaining control. It frees your ability to meet life as it unfolds and to learn, adapt, and create something meaningful out of what comes.

Redefine what makes you valuable: not your achievements, but your capacity to be present and to dance with life in each moment. Identify the times you answered life's call to change and recognize it as an ongoing process. The sooner you answer the call, the quicker problems that need solving become questions to be answered.

Focus on who you are being while you are doing. Don't rush into action without inner alignment. Integrate the being and the doing. This is you flowing as a whole person. Anchor yourself in values and principles, not outcomes. When life shakes your sense of identity, return to the solid core within you—your guiding principles that stand firm when everything else shifts.

When life changes test your resolve, use the Five Attitudes to gain clarity and respond effectively. For example:

- What would inner responsibility look like here? (Responsibility)
- What design do you choose to live by? What action steps honor your choice? (Proactivity)
- How are you contributing to the situation? Whose contribution can you invite? (Interdependence)
- How can you shift to an OK place for effectiveness? What is the deeper message you're hearing? How can you build on that and make yourself heard? (Influence)

At Excellence, your self-worth is simply defined by your willingness to meet life as it is and as it unfolds.

X2: Direction inspired by the big picture

Life changes. So do you. Even if your big picture remains relatively stable, how you live it naturally evolves. Return to your Big Picture Personal Canvas regularly. Take time to reflect. Once a week, check in: how did you bring it to life? Are any adjustments needed? This isn't just a concept; it's a source of energy and guidance, especially in times of complexity or uncertainty.

Set your priorities based on direction, not pressure. If you find yourself constantly fighting fires instead of preventing them, it indicates an urge to act without alignment or long-term vision. Allow space for realignment or course correction. Even the best direction can drift under the pressure of distraction, fatigue, or crisis. Excellence lies in your ability to course-correct with grace. Sometimes, slowing down is the fastest way forward.

X3: Courage in action

Redefine courage as aligned action, not fearlessness. Ask:

- What matters more than my comfort right now?
- What am I willing to stand for even when it costs me something?

Spot the "rational-lies." This is where Excellence loops back into Responsibility. Catch yourself when you're discounting a problem, its significance, change possibilities, or your personal abilities.[37] Ask, "What am I discounting? What truth am I overlooking here?" Consider what you would have done if you had known you wouldn't fail. Fear aside, think what your life is calling for, and how you would answer that calling if you were at your best?

Fear, like any emotion, has physical symptoms and thought patterns. Check the Emotional section in Chapter Two to process both aspects. Strengthen your inner resilience by consistently engaging in intentional life learning, recovery practices, and self-regulation tools. Courage is your ally when you deliberately step beyond your comfort zone to learn, grow, and make a meaningful impact. Acknowledge yourself for every courageous thought, word, or action you made in alignment with your Big Picture Personal Canvas. The more you spot it within yourself, the faster it grows.

Remember, courage alone is not enough. Align your actions with your big picture and your inner compass. Every week, while checking alignment with your Big Picture Personal Canvas, take note of three things you did this week that required courage, even if they were small, messy, or private.

Using The Way of the Catalyst framework

There is a striking image circulating online that has drawn the attention of psychologists and behavioral change experts. It is a powerful visual metaphor for the false restraints that so often hold us back. In the image, a horse stands still, tied to a flimsy plastic chair lying loosely on the ground. With its immense strength, the horse could break free in an instant. Yet, it doesn't move—not because the chair poses a real barrier, but because of what the horse learned early on.

Young horses are often tied to immovable objects like sturdy posts or metal rings. They pull and resist, until, after repeatedly failing to break free, they surrender. Over time, they stop questioning the restraint. Eventually, even if they are tied to something easily breakable, the mere sight or feel of being tethered is enough to keep them in place. The restraint no longer needs to be real—belief does the job.

The same thing happens in our lives, often without us realizing. What limits us is rarely the actual circumstance, but our internalized beliefs about what we can or cannot be, do, or have. Although our freedom, like our time and energy, is limited, it is still enough to create the meaningful change our heart desires. If you're not fully satisfied with, or at least accepting of, every area in your life, there's room for growth. Denial is not a strategy. The rope may not be real, but the impact is.

So the question becomes: What restraints have you stopped questioning? Dare to question the truth of those restraints. Work with what is immediately available to you—the small, simple thing you can do differently today. Your intention, determination, and commitment carry power that can unlock possibilities you hadn't seen before.

Once you've created your Big Picture Personal Canvas, there are two ways to use the Way of the Catalyst framework to guide your transformation: start from the beginning or start where you are.

Start from the beginning

Dedicate one month to integrating each trait, starting with R1. Within twelve months, you'll have embodied the core attitudes of Responsibility, Proactivity, Interdependence, and Influence.

Celebrate the small wins. Reflect on your weekly progress. Each day, take a moment to appreciate at least one thing.

Excellence—the fifth attitude—is the crown of the Catalyst. Unlike the first four, which become second nature through intentional practice, Excellence is not a destination. It's a remembrance of your inner power. It is an ongoing expansion that invites you to stay consciously responsive, anchored, aligned, and courageous, moment to moment.

Start where you are

Take the free online Culture Catalyst Self-Assessment: www.maisalhasan.com/culture-catalyst-program

The Culture Catalyst Self-Assessment features fifteen reflection statements—one for each of the fifteen catalytic traits that make up the Five Attitudes of the Catalyst.

This tool is designed to help you assess your perceived level of proficiency, both overall and within each attitude. It offers a starting point for identifying your current strengths and opportunities for growth along your personal and relational transformation journey.

Reflect on:

- Which attitudes appear to be your current strengths? How do they show up in your daily life?
- Which attitudes scored lower? What beliefs or habits might be contributing to that?
- Choose one area of growth. What small change could you begin practicing this week?

Keep integrating small, intentional shifts each week. Allow about three months to fully embody each attitude. Make it a fun and meaningful journey that is easy for you and those around you.

The Way of the Catalyst is not a path you follow; it's a way to live, moment by moment, choice by choice. Let the next step be yours—informed, intentional, and alive.

Conclusion

By now, you've journeyed through the Catalyst's fundamentals—answering the call for change and the Big Picture Personal Canvas—and the Five Attitudes of the Catalyst. These are not just abstract ideals but living practices. You've witnessed them in action through real people, in real moments—ordinary people who took the raw clay life handed them and shaped it into art, touching others' lives, sometimes through inspiration and momentum, and sometimes by driving change with ease, peace, and grace.

Let us revisit the Five Attitudes of the Catalyst.

A reminder of the Five Attitudes of the Catalyst

1. **Responsibility:** Taking charge of inner thoughts, emotions, and stories
   - R1 – Awareness of emotional states and their impact
   - R2 – Mastery in selecting emotions for effectiveness
   - R3 – Making a life-affirming choice every time
2. **Proactivity:** Living life by design
   - P1 – Recognizing one's own role in creating possibilities
   - P2 – Taking action by conscious choice
   - P3 – Demonstrating inner resilience
3. **Interdependence:** Sharing power with all involved
   - I1 – Confidence in oneself
   - I2 – Comfort with vulnerability
   - I3 – Accepting of differences
4. **Influence:** Causing an effect without force
   - F1 – Navigating disarray in oneself and others
   - F2 – Creating effective safe spaces
   - F3 – Tailoring communication to the listener

5. **Excellence:** Bringing the dynamic self, moment to moment
   - X1 – Self-worth anchored in responsiveness to change
   - X2 – Direction inspired by the big picture
   - X3 – Courage in action

If there's one insight to carry forward, it's this: meaningful change, whether in your own life or in the world around you, begins with your attitudes. It starts by taking charge of your inner world—your thoughts and emotions, and the stories you tell yourself about yourself, others, and life as a whole. Meaningful change continues to unfold when you choose to live by design, creating possibilities, making conscious choices, and building inner resilience along the way.

When it comes to others, you share power not by shrinking or dominating but by recognizing and accepting your own truth and theirs, without judgment. You relate with confidence and compassion, collaborate with integrity, and embrace differences as a collective strength. You create psychological safety, navigate misalignments, and communicate with care.

Crowning it all is your ability to stay responsive, moment by moment, anchored in a sense of self-worth that comes from within, guided by your big picture, and expressed with clarity, alignment, and courage.

Your attitudes shift, and so does the world's response to you. You don't just cope with change, you create it. Your Big Picture Personal Canvas is the compass that orients you. It brings coherence to your choices, focus to your energy, and meaning to your momentum. You stop scattering yourself in countless directions and begin moving with intent and purpose toward what truly matters.

This isn't a transformation that arrives with fireworks or dramatic breakthroughs; it's subtle, steady, and progressive, built through small but consistent shifts. It's not about becoming someone new overnight; it's about returning to who you already are, at your best, and choosing to live from that place more often. You don't need a wake-up call or the perfect time. There's no finish line, only deeper levels of awareness, alignment, and impact.

Take what resonates. Make it your way. Keep going, forward, upward, and inward. Grow by choice, not by noise.

Notes

1 "Catalyst," Merriam-Webster.com, www.merriam-webster.com/dictionary/catalyst, accessed November 3, 2024
2 Soho Voices, "The new Škoda Fabia attention test 1," YouTube (July 23, 2015), www.youtube.com/watch?v=FzJXTdDfpuQ, accessed July 18, 2025
3 T.J. DeLong, "Three questions for effective feedback," *Harvard Business Review* (August 4, 2011), https://hbr.org/2011/08/three-questions-for-effective-feedback, accessed August 3, 2025
4 P.P. Gasparini, K.B. Vieira, and M. Dias, "Disney's Pixar animation studios acquisition case: Revitalization or trouble?" *GPH-International Journal of Social Science and Humanities Research*, 8/4 (2025), 46–57, https://doi.org/10.5281/zenodo.15365962
5 "Emotion," American Psychological Association (September 4, 2018), https://dictionary.apa.org/emotion, accessed August 3, 2025
6 D.R. Hawkins, *Letting Go: The pathway of surrender* (Hay House, 2012)

7 G. Willcox, "The Feeling Wheel: A tool for expanding awareness of emotions and increasing spontaneity and intimacy," *Transactional Analysis Journal*, 12:4 (1982), 274–276, https://doi.org/10.1177/036215378201200411
8 J. Bolte Taylor, *My Stroke of Insight: A brain scientist's personal journey* (Viking Press, 2006)
9 S.B. Karpman, "Fairy tales and script drama analysis," *Transactional Analysis Bulletin*, 7:26 (1968), 39–43
10 Z. Ziglar, *See You At The Top* (Pelican Publishing, 1975)
11 D. Gilbert, *Stumbling on Happiness* (Alfred A. Knopf, 2006)
12 A.W. Schiff and J. Schiff, "Passivity," *Transactional Analysis Journal*, 1:10 (1971), 71–78
13 Ibid.
14 C.B. Sullenberger, "Captain Sully's minute-by-minute description of the miracle on the Hudson" (Inc., 2019), www.youtube.com/watch?v=w6EblErBJqw, accessed August 4, 2025
15 G. Muccino, *The Pursuit of Happyness* (Columbia Pictures, 2006)
16 E. Berne, *Games People Play* (New York: Grove Press, 1964)
17 T.A. Harris, *I'm OK, You're OK* (Harper & Row, 1969)
18 R. Pausch, "The Last Lecture," Carnegie Mellon University (September 18, 2007), www.cmu.edu/randyslecture, accessed July 29, 2025
19 R. Pausch, with J. Zaslow, *The Last Lecture: Lessons in living* (Hyperion, 2008)
20 Z. Khan, Epiphany, www.epiphany-zk.com, accessed August 5, 2025
21 The Love Academy, www.theloveacademy.world, accessed August 5, 2025
22 Ibid.
23 E. Kübler-Ross, *On Death and Dying* (Macmillan, 1969)
24 G. Willcox, "The Feeling Wheel: A tool for expanding awareness of emotions and increasing spontaneity and intimacy," *Transactional Analysis Journal*, 12/4 (1982), 274–276, https://doi.org/10.1177/036215378201200411

25 Gallup, Inc., "CliftonStrengths," www.gallup.com/cliftonstrengths/en/252137/home.aspx, accessed August 5, 2025
26 Enneagram Universe, "Take the most accurate enneagram test," https://enneagramuniverse.com, August 5, 2025
27 Functional Fluency International, "Functional Fluency products," https://functionalfluency.com/products, accessed August 5, 2025
28 Egogram, "Welcome to your Egogram," https://egogram.sk/en, accessed August 5, 2025
29 John Wiley & Sons, Inc., "Everything DiSC," www.everythingdisc.com, accessed August 5, 2025
30 The Insights Group Limited, "About Insights Discovery and our products," www.insights.com, accessed August 5, 2025
31 A.W. Schiff and J. Schiff, "Passivity," *Transactional Analysis Journal*, 1:10 (1971), 71–78
32 D.W. Merrill and R.H. Reid, *Personal Styles and Effective Performance* (CRC Press, 1981)
33 M.B. Rosenberg, *Nonviolent Communication: A language of life* (PuddleDancer Press, 2015)
34 The Black Swan Group Ltd., "Guide: Three negotiator types," www.blackswanltd.com/guide-to-3-negotiator-types, accessed August 5, 2025
35 G. Chapman, *The Five Love Languages: How to express heartfelt commitment to your mate* (Northfield Publishing, 1992)
36 G. Chapman and P. White, *The 5 Languages of Appreciation in the Workplace: Empowering organizations by encouraging people* (Northfield Publishing, 2011)
37 A.W. Schiff and J. Schiff, "Passivity," *Transactional Analysis Journal*, 1:10 (1971), 71–78

Acknowledgments

This book would not exist without the presence, wisdom, and support of many people who have touched my life in ways both seen and unseen.

To my four beautiful children, Yasser, Sarah, Karam, and Yasmina: You are the heartbeat of my life. Your love and laughter kept me anchored in what matters most.

To Elisa: Your love, care, and devotion helped me raise the children and allowed me the space to do this work.

To every client, workshop participant, and leader I've had the privilege to work with: your questions, breakthroughs, and resilience were part of the inspiration behind the concepts in this book. Every exchange with you has been a gift. I've learned and grown alongside you.

To Mom and Dad, Daad and Amin: Thank you for your steady love, grounding presence, and unwavering faith in me. Your support has carried me further than words can say.

To Toufic, the father of my children: Thank you for asking me out in February 1999, for the beautiful family we share, and for continuing to be a source of strength and joy throughout the years.

To Sulaf: Thank you for the laughter, deep conversations, and incredible times we continue to share, all of which have enriched my life in many ways. I love your fierce yet gentle spirit. Your belief in me during the hardest moments helped me keep going. Thank you for holding the big picture and for holding space for me to process and reach where I am today.

To Zimmy, Sam, Gulsun, and Adrienne: you each, in your own way, held space for my voice long before I was ready to share it. You reminded me of what is possible when clarity and courage walk side by side.

To Jinan, Mayssa, and Naila: thank you for your friendship, support, and encouragement throughout the years.

To Ezer and Binu: Thank you for bringing your brilliance and commitment to life in the Culture Catalyst

Program and its assessments. Your contribution added depth and structure to the ideas in this book.

To Zimmy and Michel: Thank you for trusting me with your stories, and for showing what it looks like to live the Way of the Catalyst with depth and grace.

To those who inspired key parts of this work, including Sulaf and Belisa, your influence runs through these pages even if unnamed.

To Geraldine, Jane, Lyndsay, and Kathleen: Thank you for your care, guidance, and attention to the flow of this book, and for helping me find the rhythm of my voice as the pages took shape.

To Zaur, my tango teacher: Your insights, some taught through motion and others through words, resonated with me far beyond the dance floor. Thank you for helping me dance with life.

To Sam: Your words stayed with me: "You have a gift this world needs. You are responsible for what you do with it." Thank you for being there when I needed clarity the most.

Finally, to every soul who believed in this message when it was still a whisper, thank you. You helped me bring it to life.

The Author

Mais Alhasan is an internationally certified leadership coach, a catalyst for personal and organizational transformation, and a guide for those navigating the intersections of life, work, and change. Based in Dubai and a mother of four, she brings a powerful blend of personal mastery, relational attunement, and systemic insight to her work.

Her training spans a wide range of modalities, including strengths strategy, co-active leadership, public speaking, physical intelligence, PSYCH-K®, organizational transactional analysis, and functional fluency. Her approach combines practical, actionable tools with profound insight, supporting individuals and organizations to cultivate clarity of direction, courage in action, and meaningful progress anchored in the big picture.

Before dedicating her career to coaching and leadership development, Mais played an instrumental role in building her family's retail business from the ground up, growing the company from three people to 1,500 employees across forty outlets in under fifteen years. She led the development of operational systems, automated procedures, and human capital structures, gaining firsthand experience in the dynamics of sustainable success.

In 2018, she founded Rise Training & Development, through which she delivered high-impact programs for clients such as the Prime Minister's Office in Dubai, Shell Abu Dhabi, and Emirates Steel. She works with individuals from all walks of life—entrepreneurs, senior executives, emerging leaders, homemakers, and young adults—each bringing their own story, aspirations, and challenges. In 2023, Mais closed the company and continued her practice independently. This allowed her to invest more time in writing, traveling, and enjoying her family.

What distinguishes Mais is not only the breadth of her professional experience, but her unique ability to translate lived experience into insight, and insight into transformative action. *The Way of the Catalyst* is an invitation into that journey, distilled from decades of practice, learning, and the deep conviction that meaningful change begins within.

To learn more or to connect for individual or organizational development, visit:

🌐 www.maisalhasan.com

www.ingramcontent.com/pod-product-compliance
Ingram Content Group UK Ltd.
Pitfield, Milton Keynes, MK11 3LW, UK
UKHW020359161125
465084UK00013B/229

9 781781 339503